To Terri We
Enjoy.
Rodney
5.2.12

DESTINY

By: Father Rodney Ador Burrows

Llumina Press

ISBN: 978-1-60594-479-1 (PB)

Printed in the United States of America by Llumina Press

Library of Congress Control Number: 2010922703

This book is dedicated to the memory of my wife, the late Dorothy Eloise Burrows, who departed this life on February 13, 1992, and my daughter, the late Allyson Vanessa Burrows, who departed this life on January 26, 1992.

Foreword

As The Bahamas' High Commissioner to London and former commissioner of police of the Royal Bahamas Police Force, I am very pleased to have been invited to write the foreword for *Destiny*, written by the Reverend Father Rodney Burrows.

The publication is intended to share with the wider community his journey from humble beginnings in Inagua to New Providence, where he enlisted in the Royal Bahamas Police Force. It reflects on the opportunity that he was given to experience the rich heritage of law enforcement in The Bahamas, which continues to evolve, even as he prepares to publish his first book, where he fondly mentions his early years on the Force, and as he now serves as chaplain to the Retired Police Officers Association.

The author's love for the land of his birth is often portrayed in his humorous and witty tales that he so likes to share among his family and friends.

The book is a source of information that will be inspirational to all readers, and in particular, to young people, because it was hard work and determination that brought the author the success that he has achieved today.

I want to thank the author for his commitment and dedication in sharing his early life story, so that others may be inspired to press on with their lives despite the challenges they may encounter.

Paul H. Farquharson, QPM

Foreword

That Father Rodney Burrows has chosen to put in print the story of his life will be an important addition to our literary archive. Indeed, I am delighted to have been invited to be a part of it in this meaningful way.

Setting out, as it does, a journey from his hardscrabble beginnings on the island of Inagua, where his total legacy was good parents, good manners, and little else, and as the fifth child of sixteen siblings, there seemed little likelihood of any personal meaningful growth. However, because of the challenges of his birth and an innate desire to rise above it, he developed a skill to survive in the constant competition for food and space. He seemed to have come to the realization early in the game that hard work and personal integrity were the only antidotes to becoming lost in the crowd where mediocrity was the norm. That his employers, and no less a person than the island commissioner, recognized his talents gave loud testament to the quality of his efforts.

To rise above the social norms of his young life and to succeed in transferring his skills from the backwater of Inagua and through the ranks of the Police Force was no mean feat. To have been chosen as staff officer by three successive commissioners of police was surely due to his legendary intolerance for administrative impropriety—a standard to which his clerical colleagues can also attest today.

Ironically, in tandem with his insistence on propriety, he developed an infectious penchant for humorous storytelling, even in the pulpit, much to the dismay and frustration of his congregation's sacred entitlement to nap during his sermons.

Somewhere along the way, his life experiences brought home to him the transitory and frail nature of worldly achievement, and that knowledge caused him to leave lucrative employment for the cloistered life of the priesthood. It was perhaps a natural progression to move from the Police Force to the priesthood, from which vantage point he could cater to the needs of the less fortunate individuals on the margins of society whom he had encountered as a policeman.

The refuge of the priesthood also allows him to place a spiritual finale on an extraordinary life surrounded now by his wife, children, and grandchildren, on whom he dotes.

Carleton W. Williams, CBE

Acknowledgements

It was Mr. Thomas Merton who wrote the book *No Man Is an Island*, and more factual words have never been spoken. However, it was the late William Edward Thompson, archdeacon and rector of Saint Agnes Anglican Church, with whom I had the good fortune of serving for a number of years as his assistant, who said it best:

"All of us are standing on the shoulders of someone to get where we are today."

I truly can attest to the indisputable fact as stated by both Thomas Merton and Archdeacon Thompson, as this book would not have become a reality without the able assistance and encouragement of

my wife Barbara,
my daughters Valarie and Samantha,
my granddaughter Hillary Wallace,
my nephew Jamal Davis,
Mr. Dudley Seifert,
Dr. Earla Carey-Baines,
Mr. Vincent Wilson, and
Mrs. Rhonda Seymour.

My daughter Valarie, whose devotion to this cause is unquestionable is worthy of special commendation.

I am grateful to my cousin, former Commissioner of Police, now High Commissioner Paul Farquharson and my dear friend Carleton Williams for their encouragement and their contribution by way of the Forward.

Contents

Introduction

I commenced writing for the *Police Magazine* in 1987, at which time I was serving as the staff officer to the commissioner of police, Mr. Gerald Augustus Bartlett. Through encouragement from my fellow police officers, family members, and the public, I continued to produce articles for the magazine until my retirement from the Force in the summer of 1992.

Shortly after my retirement, I left The Bahamas to test my vocation for the Sacred Priesthood at Codrington College in Saint John, Barbados. Two years later, after successfully completing my studies, I returned home and was ordained a deacon in June 1994 and a priest one year later.

When time permitted, I continued to record my life's story, entitled *Destiny*. In recent times, I was, and still am, continually encouraged by people who have read my magazine articles to write a book, but I kept procrastinating. It has been said that nothing happens before its time, and, being a person of deep faith, I believe that.

What is the driving force behind a person who goes to the trouble to research and then write a book? Is it the thing that makes the cash register ring? In part, that may be so. But for the years that I wrote for the *Police Magazine*, I received nothing. So it can't be the money.

My main reason for recording my life's story is to encourage people, who have had what may be referred to as "a bad start in life," to know that with God's help, integrity, and devotion to hard work, he or she can make it to the top. The president of the United States of America, Mr. Barack Obama, has proven that.

My police service spanned thirty-one years, and the testing of my vocation to the present amounts to eighteen years. I was born in 1943. That is a lot of mileage, which means that one volume will not do justice to my biography. Therefore, I shall write two volumes spanning my police career and one volume on my vocation to the Sacred Priesthood.

Book one will chronicle my birth to my boarding a British Overseas Airways Corporation (BOAC) airplane in London for the voyage home after completing a course in Hendon, England. It may be termed *interesting*.

Book two will chronicle my return to New Providence in February 1973 from Hendon, England, to 1992. It may be termed *extraordinary*.

Book three will chronicle the years 1992 to 2010. It may be termed *unbelievable*.

My Beginnings

I, Rodney Ador Burrows, was born on February 11, 1943, to the parents of James and Fericeta Burrows in Matthew Town, Inagua, the southernmost island of The Bahamas archipelago. My great grandfather, Isaiah of Long Island, begot my grandfather, Benjamin of Scrub Hill, Long Island, and Benjamin married Emma Farquharson of Pompey Bay, Acklins. It was from this union that my father, James Gaston, first saw the light of day. When my father was nine years old, his mother died and he went to Acklins Island to live with his uncle, Dougal Farquharson. Dougal was the owner and captain of a large sailing sloop that plied between Acklins, Cuba, and Haiti, with regular stops at Inagua for the purpose of trading in provisions. James often went along for the ride.

At the age of nineteen on one such trip, James disembarked at Inagua, and eight years later on July 21, 1937, he married Fericeta Hall of Matthew Town. Fericeta's father, Elijah, hailed from Lorimers, one of the islands in the Turks and Caicos. He had migrated to Inagua in search of employment with the Salt Company, the production of salt being a major industry in The Bahamas at that time. Elijah married Ethel Roker of Matthew Town, and that union was responsible for my mother, Fericeta, coming into existence. My parents believed, according to some fairy tale, that children were poor people's wealth. Consequently, they increased the population of Inagua to the tune of sixteen, of which I, Rodney Ador, was the fifth. Over the years, I've been asked about the name *Ador,* and I have come to the conclusion that my parents were beginning to run out of names, even after only the fifth birth.

At the age of eight, my mother was adopted by a woman named Catherine Mackey and her husband Charles as her mother was sick. Charles sold charcoal for a living while Catherine did midwifery. My eldest brother, Charles Alexander, was also adopted by the Mackeys and a part of my boyhood days was spent at that address. I vividly recall accompanying Catherine at nights with a flashlight and a basket over my shoulder with bush medicine and other paraphernalia after a messenger would summon her to deliver a baby. The messenger would say, "Ma Cathy, Momma [or my wife] has taken in to have baby."

On our arrival at the home, I remained outside, and for hours, I would kill mosquitoes until a baby started screaming. Shortly thereafter, Catherine would appear with the news of the baby's gender. The going price for a delivery varied, and to this day, it still baffles me. If it was a boy, she collected one pound, the equivalent of three U.S. dollars; the going cost for a girl was fifteen shillings, the equivalent of three-quarters of a pound. I was extremely disappointed when it was a girl, because Catherine would only give me one shilling if she delivered a girl. If she delivered a boy, she would give me two shillings. While waiting on the baby's arrival, I would pray fervently for it to be a boy.

There were also times when I received no payment because of the baby's demise. Momma Cathy, as she was affectionately called, would emerge from the house and say, "Son, I lost that one this time." I suppose like everything else in life, you win some and you lose some; but that was no consolation to me. There were also times when the families, because of poverty, were unable to pay the cost of the delivery. In such instances, Catherine would say, "Son, God will provide. He surely does; but those words were of little or no comfort to me. I expected her to be paid for services rendered. There were also other occasions when I was paid up to four shillings to bury the baby. I would secure a shoe box for a coffin, and with the cover of darkness, I would do my thing. It is true that as a boy I was afraid of cemeteries, but between fright, poverty, and money, fright was ranked a distant third.

My father was a short thin man with what Bahamians would call "sharp" features and straight hair. He was independent and was not one to suffer fools gladly; neither did he mince his words. I vividly recall one occasion when I was sent to collect a drill my father had lent to a friend. On the way home, the drill was taken from me by Mr. Jim Erickson, one of the owners of the Salt Company. The following morning, my father approached Jim Erickson in the presence of his employees and shouted, "You white son of a bitch! What you did to my son yesterday, you should have tried that with me! They would have been burying you this morning." Those were some of the nicer words my father used. I was afraid that his failure to mince his words *and* his determination to speak his mind would result in him being arrested and jailed. At that time, to address a white person in that manner meant trouble. The drill was still in the back of Mr. Erickson's truck. So my father removed it and walked away saying, "In the future, if you let any son of a bitch take anything from you, I will disown you as my son."

Besides not mincing his words, my father was an honest, hardworking man. When there was money to be made to support his family, he readily performed. He was a jack-of-all-trades but mastered none. Of course, you could not have told him that, for he would have been gravely offended. As I recall, the last major job he contracted was the construction of a wall around Saint Philip's Anglican Church on Inagua with my godfather, Joseph "Dodie" Balfour, as his deputy. As Dodie and reading were not friends, and my father was slightly cross-eyed, the job turned out to be a disaster. You could have literally hidden in some of the valleys in that wall. Father McConall, the rector of Saint Philip's at the time, said, "Gentlemen, with that job, God is not pleased. A nine and a half months pregnant woman must have held that tape during the time of measurements."

My mother was a solidly built, intelligent, honest, and hardworking woman, who was approximately five feet eight inches in height. She worked equally as hard as my father on the farm and washed clothes for Mrs. Marjorie Erickson and her family. Additionally, she had the sole responsibility of the day-to-day management of the family affairs, as my father was seldom at home. She was sufficiently educated to assist her children with their schoolwork. Her favourite sayings were, "We are very poor," "You must not beg," and "For God's sake, you must not steal!" More of her famous sayings were, "Poorness is no disgrace, it's only a put back," "One day pig will grow into hog," "When you are down, the only way for you to go is up," "Trust in God." "By the sweat of your brow, you shall eat bread." I shall forever cherish those everlasting words, as my mother passed away at the young age of fifty-six, however my father lived on to celebrate the seventy-eighth anniversary of his birth. May both their souls rest in peace!

As I was the fifth child in a family with sixteen, I came to the early realization that *work* must be my watchword if I were to succeed in life. As a lad, I performed just about every manual task imaginable. My parents were farmers, and on Inagua, a salt-producing island with little rainfall, very little food was harvested. My attendance at Inagua Public School was erratic, as I often suffered with that terrible complaint called "migraine," which only the sufferer is able to describe.

An ordinary day, that is, a day when I was not struck with that dreaded complaint, started at five a.m. with the toting of water and firewood or any number of chores. At nine a.m., I was given a piece of bread, a roasted potato or some flour pap, sometimes with sugar, and was told to hurry and run to school, where, upon arrival, I received a daily whipping for lateness. I was also faced with a dilemma once I got to school: begging a leaf of paper on which to record the day's lesson and a piece of pencil with which to write it. The headmaster would question me regarding my purpose for even coming to school because of my continuous tardiness and my failure to have the appropriate school supplies. I would return home for lunch at noon, where a bun, when available, would be served. Much work awaited me at three p.m. on my return from school, like grinding Indian corn. I disliked the chore because it gave me calluses and my hands would remain sore for long periods; however, my mother thought it was my specialty. Dinner was eventually served between seven and eight p.m. After dinner, I was told to say my prayers and sleep wherever I may, except the kitchen, where there were rodents, and my parents' bedroom, for obvious reasons. I was annoyed on wash days because no dirty clothes were left on which to place my head. On those days, I slept on a crocus sack on the floor.

Although we did not have much and our house was very small, my mother insisted that it be kept clean. My sisters were required to assist with household chores including scrubbing the wooden floor, cooking and baking. We had an outside kitchen and meals were prepared on an open wood fire. Like me, my brothers had to assist with the toting of water, collecting firewood as well as helping to care for our animals.

We had our fun times and as there was no money to purchase toys, we often resorted to making our own like spinning tops, which we made from the trunk and limbs of the lignum vitae tree. Shooting marbles was also a part of our recreation. We were fortunate in that we were given marbles by neighbours and we also won marbles off other children.

At the age of ten, I was gainfully employed as a houseboy by one of the three Erickson brothers, the owners of the Salt Company. The Ericksons were very kind to me and ordered that I be fed a glass of Carnation powdered milk and a peanut butter sandwich daily. This diet gave me diarrhea at first, as I had never consumed such a meal. My brothers and sisters would laugh at my discomfort and say that the food was too rich for my blood. Along with the food, I received a weekly salary of ten shillings for my service, which I always gave to my mother to help with family expenses. This was supplemented with monies earned from performing part-time work at various business establishments and using my father's donkey and cart to deliver provisions from the local mail boat. There were even times when I was required to go around Matthew Town selling crawfish and field produce on my head in a box.

While on one such round selling bananas, I called at a barroom where my attention was drawn to a Victrola record player that was playing a record entitled *Mama Lend Me Your Pigeon to Keep Company with Mine*. I was startled, to say the least, at hearing words and music and not seeing the artist. In my endeavour to ascertain what was happening, I rested the box with the bananas on the bar counter and went to where the record player stood. I asked the proprietor where the man was who was singing. He replied, "He is in the box."

I answered, "He must be a small fellow."

Still not fully understanding what was happening, I decided to continue on my journey, only to find banana skins where once lay two dozen ripe bananas. Without the bananas or money, I returned home, where I was soundly whipped and sent to collect the donkey and sheep.

My time with the Ericksons was pleasant, and I received steady increases in my salary. However, I was required to resign as houseboy when I turned fourteen. It was the standard practice that on attaining the age of fourteen years, the services of boys were terminated. The Ericksons had very beautiful daughters and that may have been the reason for not keeping houseboys beyond the age of fourteen.

Mr. Jim Erickson was a hard worker. Some Saturdays, he and I would commence work at noon and work well into the night. On one such occasion, while erecting a fence, the rain came and he insisted that we complete the task. I agreed and arrived home soaked from the rain. My mother became furious and questioned my stupidity for working in the rain. She wanted to know if Jim Erickson was going to take care of me if I got sick! I told her that Mr. Erickson had worked in the rain as well. She became even more furious and replied, "Boy, don't be an ass. Don't you know that white people head is waterproof?"

When I left the Ericksons' employ, I went to work at the Inagua General Store. My new employment got me a change in my mode of dress. Cotton shirts replaced those made from flour bags bearing the words, "Excellent for cakes and pastries. Milled in Canada." Khaki trousers took the place of grits sacks bearing the inscription, "Produced from the finest grains Canada has to offer." I was also afforded the luxury of wearing tennis shoes for the first time, and, may I hasten to add, they were carefully looked after. My weekly salary was £3.18.0, about $11.50.

I was very happy at my new place of employment and looked forward to new challenges as I gained confidence. My first assignment was the Herculean task of loading and off-loading bulk groceries from a truck whenever the Ericksons' boats arrived. The provisions were then priced and placed on shelves. I was then made to fill orders and assist with deliveries. After three months of stocking inventory, filling and delivering orders, I was assigned the job of making ice cream. The company had just taken delivery of a new machine that became my toy.

Poverty had deprived me of such luxuries, so I welcomed the opportunity to operate such a magnificent piece of equipment. My stay at producing ice cream was short-lived, however, as I moved from the stock room to the general store after two months.

I was completely confused when I was assigned to work in the meat and vegetable department. Serving meats, such as chicken wings, thighs, whole chicken, and pig's feet, were simple. The problem came when customers ordered items like chuck roast, T-bone steak, veal, and the like.

The dry goods section, where I was posted next, was the biggest obstacle of all. It was in this section that I learned how terrible I was at using a pair of scissors. Women by the droves returned material that I had cut like the jib of a sailboat. This posting was also an embarrassment for those women who wanted to purchase underwear. So, for the reasons given above, I was eventually posted to the canned goods section.

Shortly after the latter posting, I was seconded to a salt ship named after one of Mr. Jim Erickson's daughters, *Cecile Erickson*. This vessel transported salt from Inagua to Brunswick, Georgia. The voyage, if I remember correctly, lasted between two and a half to three days. At first I became seasick like a dog, but eventually things began to improve. Aboard ship, a sailor was required to perform OJ, or odd jobs, such as scrubbing the deck, steering the vessel, washing down paint, greasing cables, chipping rust, and painting. The life of a sailor was not a pleasant one, and I looked forward to the end of my second trip.

My return to serving groceries was very much welcomed, and after a short while, I received a one hundred percent increase in my salary. But the trips to the outside world opened my eyes, and it was then that I realized how important travelling to other parts of the world could be.

Shortly after my seventeenth birthday, I came to know the new district commissioner, Mr. Herbert Cleveland Walkine, who had recently arrived in Inagua. He would come to the store and ask that I fill his orders and deliver the groceries to his vehicle, where I would be given a shilling. This practice went on for about four months before I was summoned to his office by Lance Corporal Randolph Worrell.

Employment Opportunities

When I arrived at his office, Commissioner Walkine said, "Rodney, I have been watching you since my arrival here and you have impressed me with your general conduct. You are wasting your time and talent in Inagua. I suggest that you go into Nassau and seek employment!"

I said, "Thank you, sir. But what will I do in Nassau?"

He replied, "Join the Police Force."

After a further discussion, I left his office with an application form and with the intention of enlisting as a police officer. My good friend, Mr. Rudolph Cunningham, was also given an application form and we both agreed to submit them.

From the outset, my mother was against my enlisting in the Police Force. On the day of my departure for Nassau, she cried profusely. I remember her saying, "Son, you are going to Nassau where those crazy people beat up policemen, and when I listen, you will be dead." With those words she handed me an envelope, kissed me, and said, "God be with you, and behave yourself."

With a heavy heart and a thousand things racing through my mind, I pondered whether I was making the right decision. My mother's worries, I thought, were twofold: one, she worried about the loss of my income; and two, she feared for my well-being as a policeman. My father had very little to say in respect to my decision. He only asked that I be careful.

Miriam
DECEASED
Winston
Ural
Eddington
Brenda
James Sr.
DECEASED
Aiden
James Jr.
Gloria
Emily
Adrian
DECEASED
Charles
DECEASED

MY FAMILY

The Inaugural Voyage

After kissing my loved ones goodbye, and near tears, I left my place of residence and boarded the MV *Air Pheasant* for the long journey to New Providence.

Keeping my appointment with destiny, I sat quietly beside my suitcase on the deck of my transportation, staring out at the Inagua General Store. Finally, at three p.m., on Friday, February 17, 1961, anchor was weighed, and after three long blasts of the ship's whistle, we were on our way.

I remained in my position until I could no longer see my treasured island. Then I enquired from my uncle, who was a steward on the boat, where I was to sleep. He inspected my ticket and escorted me down a flight of stairs to the bottom of the vessel and into an open area that resembled an open ward at the Princess Margaret Hospital.

Pointing to one of the bunk beds, he said, "Rodney, take the top one, because if you sleep on the bottom one, and the person on the top gets seasick, some of the vomit will come on you." Then he said, "Plus, every time the person on top has to come down, he will have to put his big foot on the edge of your bed, and if you sleep too close to the edge, you would get mashed." Thanking Uncle Frankie for his advice, I placed my suitcase in a corner and sat on the bed assigned to me. Before ascending the stairs to the upper deck, Uncle Frankie promised to return with more tips on how I could cope with life over the next three days in my new surroundings.

In a relatively short period, people bearing second-class tickets and suitcases began to fill the room. Women with small children and older men were assigned bottom bunks, while men and boys occupied those on the top. Among the elderly passengers were two old men who constantly smoked their pipes and were regular users of the only bathroom available to second-class passengers. They would go into the bathroom and remain there for what seemed to be an hour or more, only to find a long queue at the door on their return. It was later discovered that both men were travelling to New Providence to consult a physician about their bladder problems. It is safe to assume that when the need arose for them to urinate, one could not start and the other could not stop.

The MV *Air Pheasant* was a long and narrow boat that rolled heavily when confronted with heavy seas. Passengers had to stand erect, hold tightly on to the beds, plant their feet firmly on the floor, and walk slowly between rolls when they wanted to move about. Normally passengers only left their beds when it was absolutely necessary.

As the sun began to set, I went to the deck in search of my uncle, from whom, naturally, I expected to be given preferential treatment. I was disappointed, however, when he told me that the second-class passengers were fed only when the first-class passengers were through eating. I was further informed that there was only one kitchen; therefore, the first-class passengers were served peas and rice and pork chops with dessert, while the second-class passengers were served peas and grits and corned beef with no dessert. The word "dessert" was not in my vocabulary, so I enquired as to its meaning. Frankie informed me that it was "something sweet they does give you to eat when you done eat" and that it was served to the first-class passengers and not the second-class passengers and crew.

By that time, I had become very hungry, and as a result of not having had lunch, I became persistent in my efforts to secure food. Again, I petitioned Uncle Frankie to arrange something for me to eat. He promised to see what he could do. Finally, about fifteen minutes later, he appeared with a coffee can filled with peas and rice and pork chops. He asked that I get lost somewhere to eat it because Captain Lockhart was a funny man and would fire him if he got caught. I am certain that I broke a record with the time it took me to devour that meal. Frankie, I thought, was now behaving like a true uncle, and as such, he went up a few notches in my estimation. When the corned beef and grits came around, I joyfully received my entitlement.

The night passed quietly without incident. The only sound came from the Caterpillar engines that propelled the ever-rocking *Air Pheasant* on its way toward Crooked Island.

Bright and early the next morning, the vessel dropped anchor off Crooked Island. The dinghy, laden with freight and a mailbag, was lowered into the water for the residents of that impoverished land. Drums of kerosene were also thrown into the sea and towed to shore. The process took about two hours to complete. On the dinghy's return, passengers with luggage, field produce, and empty oil drums were taken aboard. Inquiries revealed that the weather had been too rough to land the freight on the vessel's journey to Inagua. When the task of unloading the dinghy was completed and the small boat was once again on board, with three sharp blasts of the ship's whistle, we were once again ocean bound. This time en route to Clarence Town, Long Island.

Once on the way, the crew began serving breakfast to passengers with higher status. The fortunate had a choice of ham or bacon, eggs, cereal, toast, and cheese, while the unfortunate ones received sausage and grits with tea. The first-class passengers also enjoyed the comfort of eating at tables in a proper dining room. Everyone else either ate on the ship's deck or in the hole where they slept.

Even though I had only paid "beer" money for my passage, I had developed a "champagne" appetite. So I went in search of Uncle Frankie.

"Rodney!" Frankie said in answer to my plea for better food. "This is morning, and the captain does be all over the place. But I will see what I can do." I told him to bring it to the bow of the boat where I would be waiting.

I had a long wait. I thought that I had been forgotten, when I suddenly heard, "Rodney!"

"Here I am," I said, "what all you bring?"

Frankie said, "Here, take this and eat it quick," while handing me a coffee can. This time the contents were ham, scrambled eggs, bacon, sausages, and toast. As before, I got lost behind the ship's dinghy where I ate the food to my heart's content. Frankie, I thought, was the greatest. I complimented him highly when he returned some thirty minutes later with a plate of yellow grits and sausage in one hand and a mug of tea in the other.

The journey to Long Island was pleasant, and with the seas being calm, many of the passengers chose to lounge around the deck talking to one another. While conversing with a young man who had joined the ship at Crooked Island, I was greeted by a man I knew, a Mr. Chestnut, the owner of a luxury yacht. Inagua had been a stop on his itinerary for well over seven years and he had visited the Inagua General Store on many occasions, and would have none other than me fill his orders. He had also consistently asked me to join him in the United States where he owned a chain of restaurants. On this occasion, he reported that his yacht had developed engine trouble. Because he had to attend an urgent meeting in Philadelphia on the coming Tuesday, he had decided to travel on the *Air Pheasant*.

Mr. Chestnut took our chance meeting as an opportunity to renew his request that I join his staff in the United States. He also tried to discourage me from enlisting in the Force with tales of how dangerous the job of a policeman was. I may have acceded to his request if not for the fact that I had given my word to Commissioner Walkine to enlist with the Force. You see, I was taught that a man's word was his honour, and not to honour one's word would make him less than a man.

Mr. Chestnut gave me his address and telephone number before he departed and asked that I reconsider his offer. There was a time when I did consider taking him up on it, but it was not destined to be.

Having been left alone after the departure of Mr. Chestnut to his prestigious first-class cabin, I was once again joined by my newly-made friend from Crooked Island, Ezekiel. Like me, he too was travelling to New Providence in search of a better way of life. Our reason for journeying to Nassau was similar to that of Dick Whittington, who, in that famous *Royal Reader* fable, journeyed to London after being told that the streets were paved with gold and who became wealthy with the aid of a cat. But I did not find Nassau to be the same and neither did my friend Ezekiel, who did not tarry long in Nassau. He is now living somewhere in Long Island, New York.

Just after dusk, the *Air Pheasant* berthed at Clarence Town, Long Island, the birthplace of my father. On completion of the business transactions there, the ship slipped its mooring and was once again on the high seas headed for the final stop. This time, however, the sea was rough and the *Air Pheasant* danced to the heavy tune of the angry waves. Passengers without strong legs retired to their bunks and many plates of food were passed along to those with strong stomachs, one of whom was my friend from Crooked Island. At the day's end, I was obliged to ask whether Zeke had ever eaten bologna sausage before this voyage, because, for each passenger who refused his or her meal, Zeke requested and ate the sausage from their plates. He also requested and received additional slices of sausage from the kitchen. I concluded that one of two things must have happened to Zeke: either he was deprived of sausage while growing up or he had heard that the company producing the commodity was going out of business. It is my hope that Zeke, by now, has had his fill of sausage.

New Beginnings

Despite the roughness of the sea, spirits were high the next morning for we were to set foot on New Providence. As promised by the captain, at ten thirty a.m., on Sunday, February 19, 1961, I stepped ashore at George Roberts Dock with all my possessions in a brown suitcase that I clutched tightly in my hand.

When we landed, I was expecting to be greeted and collected by a member of the Police Force. After waiting for an hour, by which time my fellow passengers had left, I went in search of Uncle Frankie. I found him on board carrying out his tasks. He said that he was still on duty, so he was unable to leave. It was then that I told him my reason for being in Nassau. I had kept my mission a secret because if I was unsuccessful in my quest to join the Force, I would have to return to Inagua and report to my old job.

Eventually, one of Uncle Frankie's friends took me to the Police Headquarters on East Street where I explained my reason for being in Nassau to the officer-in-charge at the Main Guard. The officer was pleasant, but he informed me that he had no instructions or knowledge of my arrival. He advised me to return Monday when the office would be open. I thanked him and left the guard room a confused man. Then Uncle Frankie's friend deposited me at the home of another uncle, who shall remain nameless for obvious reasons, as you will learn.

I was made to feel welcome at my temporary place of abode. When I opened the envelope my mother had given me, I discovered one hundred pounds (about three hundred U.S. dollars) and my life insurance policy with Star Insurance Company. It was the first time I had ever opened an envelope containing monies belonging to me, and I felt a sense of maturity. Previously, I had delivered all the monies I had earned to my mother intact. She would then give me a few shillings to buy, according to her, "foolishness." My uncle, who was unemployed, had sent his family to Long Island to reside with his wife's parents until employment came along. At least that was what he told me. As a result of his plight, I offered him five pounds (about fifteen dollars), which he gratefully accepted.

As instructed, on Monday, February 20, 1961, I visited the Depot and Training School recruiting office at Police Headquarters where I met Corporal Dudley Cromwell Seifert and Constable Charles Nelson Stubbs. Seifert informed me that a letter announcing my arrival was on file but that it did not specify a date and time. Depot commandant, Mr. George C. Lavell, was consulted. He ordered that I be tested physically and on my educational background to determine my suitability for police service. At the end of my tests, I was instructed to return the following Monday for my results.

My uncle was waiting for me outside of Police Headquarters. As he was unemployed, my uncle and I walked to and from his home. We stopped at a Chinese store where I was made to purchase vegetable soup, sausage, bread, and two bottles of soda. This was to be our lunch and dinner for the duration of my stay at his address. The exception was Sunday when we both dined on white rice and pork chops, purchased, as usual, with my money.

Overcoming the "Height" Challenge

As instructed, I returned the following Monday to keep my appointment with Corporal Seifert. I was happy on being told of my success at both examinations, but I soon became sad on learning that I was half an inch too short for the Force. I assured Corporal Seifert that I was a growing boy, so I should be given the chance to grow the half inch. I recommended that if nature was not kind to me in the growing department, then at the end of my six-month training period I should be discharged. To this, Seifert laughed and enquired whether I could play a musical instrument. Jokingly, I told him that the only thing I could play was the fool. Again he laughed. Then he informed me that the Force was already in possession of many such people. I told him that one more would make little or no difference.

Next, he asked me to produce my educational certificates and advised me to prepare to see the commandant. I told Seifert of my willingness to meet the commandant but that I was not the custodian of even a health certificate. Ten minutes later, Commandant George Lavell informed me that because of my failure to meet the Force's requirements, along with my inability to play an instrument, which would have enabled me to play in the band, my services could not be entertained. To me, these were words of despondency. I begged to be given a chance. Mr. Lavell told me that the Force was governed by rules and regulations; he was sorry, but his hands were tied.

As I was about to exit the commandant's office, he said, "I tell you what, I am going to request that Commissioner

Walkine at Inagua submit a report on your conduct and suitability for the Force. Come back sometimc next week!" To me, those words were comforting. I thanked him for his efforts in granting me further consideration, for I felt confident that Mr. Walkine would submit a favourable report on my behalf.

Unsavory Characters I Met While Roaming the Streets of Nassau

My uncle, who had accompanied me for the second time to Police Headquarters, left me after suggesting that I try to learn a bit about Nassau on my own. This, of course, he said after relieving me of another ten pounds (thirty dollars). He promised to pay me back, but some forty-nine years have passed and this has yet to happen.

From Police Headquarters, I walked south on East Street in the vicinity of Kemp's Liquor Store, where I met three of my homeboys. We were happy to see one another, and they invited me to join them at an apartment on the second floor of the building east of Kemp's Liquor Store.

While there, I was introduced to a middle-aged man called "Rev." I concluded from our first meeting that Rev was a shady character. He reminded me of the Artful Dodger character from *Oliver Twist*. Rev was an American who drove a very large American car. His place of residence, it appeared, catered to all and sundry, for men and women were coming and going at will. It did not take me long to conclude that I was in the wrong company, so I left at the first opportunity.

One of my homeboys followed me down the stairs where he requested a loan of five pounds (fifteen dollars). His parents in Inagua were supposed to send his allowance by the next mail, which had yet to arrive.

Continuing my journey toward my uncle's, I met another one of my homeboys near Quakoo Street. He greeted me with, "Rodney, what this I hear about you joining the Force? You mean that's the best thing you can do? You mean you travelled all that distance to have people make a fool out of you?" I asked him his reason for saying what he did. He told me that sensible people did not join the Police Force. Somewhat distressed, I continued on my way and felt proud for being able to find home on my own.

My uncle arrived home an hour after I did, and I told him about my day. The following morning, my uncle said, "Rodney, you know, Nassau is a dangerous place, and you should not be walking around with all that money in your pocket. You should give it to me to put in the bank." With this advice, I readily agreed and gave him fifty pounds to deposit on my behalf. But the bank where he deposited my money must have disappeared after he made that initial deposit, because every time I requested my bank book he would tell me that the bank had closed before he got there or some other hard-luck story. By that time, my funds were getting low and I had no source on which to draw to refurbish the stock. It became necessary for me to readjust and govern my life accordingly. As a result, I was obliged to drop the vegetable soup from my daily diet and settle for bread and sausage, washed down by a bottle of fruit champagne soda. Like Zeke of Crooked Island, I had been deprived of such luxuries as sodas, so I had made a vow—when I became a man, I would consume all the things that had eluded me during my youth.

My days were spent roaming the streets of Nassau and eating rum raisin ice cream. While waiting the turn of the next week, I had the opportunity of being introduced to an aunt, whose name I will not mention for she did me worse than her brother, my unnamed uncle. She was like a parasite, and every time we met, which was quite regular, she would remark, "Rodney, throw me out." That was the phrase used in the sixties when one begged for money.

By the week's end, I was left with only a five pound note and my Star Life Insurance papers.

The Transition

At eight a.m. on Monday, March 6, 1961, I was greeted at the commandant's office with the news that I was to commence training on March 14, and I was to take up residence at Neville's House at Police Headquarters.

The oaths of allegiance and office were administered by Deputy Commissioner Augustus Roberts on the morning of March 14. Prior to leaving his office, Mr. Roberts asked me how much and who I paid to join the Force as he was certain that I was not the required height. He also stated that should I not grow to the required height by the time of graduation, dismissal would result.

I spent the remainder of the day collecting second- and, in some instances, third-hand uniforms from Police Stores. A careful and diligent search turned up uniforms that were too large. The officer-in-charge of Police Stores, Sergeant Ivan Brooks, told me, "You don't fit the uniform; the uniform fit you." After I had my uniforms, I was then assigned my regimental numbers—303. Willard Williams, a young man from Wemyss Bight, Eleuthera, who also enlisted that day, was given 304.

We joined the recruits of the B squad, who were already in training. They were Hazel Pratt, Laban Brice, Joseph Cox, Bernard Lundy, George Poitier, William Allen, Leon Anderson, Clifford Bullard, Alfred Williams, Whitfield Williams, Bersil Miller and Herman Fernander.

We were a happy group, and we supported one another at any cost. I was considered the odd man out because I knew nothing about the nightlife of Nassau, nor did I accompany them on their nightclub rounds. It was, and maybe still is, the attitude that if you hailed from the Family Islands, you were a novice at everything—except, of course, religion.

Despite my relatives' shabby treatment, I had the courtesy to inform them of my admittance into the Police Force. Both my aunt and uncle rejoiced at the news of my enlistment and asked me to visit them regularly, which I did, and was further taken for a ride.

I had been a member of the Third Bahamas Company of Boys Brigade in Inagua. As a member, I was taught drills similar to what was taught in the military. I also had to practice a certain amount of discipline. As the force was a semi-military organization; it was this exposure that placed me ahead of my fellow recruits in those two areas.

The first week passed quietly. At six a.m., five days a week, we were required to jog to Montagu Beach and back. Some mornings we were required to swim as well, and then we would run back to the barracks. Corporal Cyril Smith was our physical education and drill instructor. He was a master at his trade and was always willing to lend a listening ear to our many complaints. Inspector Sigfred Wilson, the depot instructor, was equally as good. Lance Corporal Malcolm McKenzie, who had served previously at Inagua, showed promise of becoming a leader. Corporal Vernon Wilkinson was an efficient drill and classroom instructor, and Commandant Lavell was approachable.

I was promised a weekly salary of twelve pounds (thirty-six dollars) when I was appointed. Food and Canteen deductions, however, dipped heavily into one's pay by week's end. If you were fortunate, you would collect maybe five or six pounds, depending, of course, on how often you visited the Canteen.

Taken Advantage of by my Aunt and Uncle

I decided to visit my aunt and uncle after receiving my fourth paycheck. On my arrival, my aunt said, "Big shot, throw me out." To be in their good graces, I gave them both a pound. My aunt said that she was starting an asue (savings plan) and that I should join. I should have learned my lesson by now, but as the saying goes, "a fool is born each day." Again, I allowed myself to be used.

The asue was to run for twelve weeks, and I was to receive the sixth draw. I was required to throw the sum of three pounds (nine dollars) per week. The sixth draw came and I requested my draw. My aunt informed me that Mrs. 'X's' mother had died, and as a result, she was given the draw. The seventh, eighth, ninth, tenth, and eleventh draws passed with similar fairy tales. When the twelfth draw was at hand, I said to my aunt, "Aunt, nobody else in the asue to die. Now it's only me left, so I come for my draw."

She replied, "Rodney, my boyfriend asked that you loan him the money, and so I gave it to him."

"But I told you I needed the money to send to my mother. She has not received anything since I came to Nassau."

She answered, "Rodney, I thought you were going to say yes, and therefore, I gave the money to my boyfriend."

I became furious and told her that whenever she received the money from her boyfriend, she was to keep it. As far as I was concerned from that day, she was no longer my aunt and her brother was no longer my uncle. It was the last time I visited either one.

The Graduation

Although I never grew to meet the height requirement, I was allowed to remain. I was considered far from being an exceptional student, but, as the saying goes, "In a country where everyone is blind, the one-eyed man is king." With a few exceptions, I could boast of being such a man; for on the day of graduation, I placed eighth out of sixteen students. I was handicapped when it came to answering general knowledge questions about New Providence. Questions like naming ten one-way streets went unanswered. On one such paper I wrote, "My name is Rodney A. Burrows, and I just arrived from Inagua."

Initially, I was told that I would be back-squadded to complete the required six months training but instead, I graduated with the others on July 16, 1961. The highlight of my graduation exercises came when an English gentleman, General Dudley Russell, spoke. He said that while serving in Palestine, he and Field Marshal Bernard Law Montgomery had a discussion over drinks of scotch and water on the question of how a true leader was measured. At the discussion's end, they both came to the same conclusion—a true soldier, and indeed, a man, must be judged on the way he handles power. Those words left an indelible impression in my memory. Those words, spoken in Africa during the World War II campaign, are as true today as they were then.

Mr. Herbert C. Walkine, former district commissioner, Inagua

Constable Rodney Burrows, Chief Justice Ralph Campbell, Constable Maxwell Lightbourne

Top Row: Earl Alleyne, Akel Clarke
Bottom Row: Nelson Stubbs, Dudley Seifert

My First Case

On Monday, July 19, 1961, at seven a.m., after enjoying the weekend off, I reported for duty at the Southern Police Station as instructed. At nine, the officer-in-charge of the Southern Division, Superintendent E. James Bryan, addressed the eight of us and instructed Sergeant George Gilbert Moncur to detail us. I was sent to work at the Cable Beach Police Station.

People of means resided at Cable Beach. Today's Lyford Cay is similar to Cable Beach of 1961. Lance Corporal Samuel Wesseling, with whom I worked, was thorough and kind. He insisted that officers who performed properly would encounter no problems from him. My first tour of duty was from seven a.m. to two p.m. and the next week it was ten p.m. to seven a.m.

I was anxious to make my first case as a young constable. At three a.m., on Tuesday, August 3, 1961, while on point at West Bay Street in front of the pink building east of the then, Ambassador Beach Hotel, I saw my first case approaching in the form of a truck being driven without lights. I stopped the truck, and with notebook and pencil in hand, I proceeded to gather information for my traffic offence report (TOR).

"Good morning, sir," I began. "Would you mind explaining your reason for driving without lights?"

"Ye-ye-ye-yes-yes, Officer. I jus-jus-jus-just come from the Nassau Beach Lodge [Hotel] to pick up hog food, and whe-whe-whe-when I ge-ge-ge-get into the tru-tru-tru-truck, I pulled the choke for the lights."

In retrospect, I now conclude that this answer merited a warning; however, at the time, I thought that I was making my first case. As such, I lost all sense of reason.

I asked, "What is your name?"

"Charles Linwood Austin," he replied. (I later found out that he was a prominent person in the community who had the award Member of the British Empire (MBE) bestowed upon him by Her Majesty, the Queen)

"Where do you live?" I asked.

"McCollough Corner, east."

"What is your occupation and place of employment?"

"Construction supervisor with Cavalier Construction Company," he said.

Prior to his departure, I warned Mr. Austin of being prosecuted for driving without his lights on. He said, "Al-al-al-all right, Officer."

I remained at my point for another fifteen minutes, and then I proceeded to my second point, which was Prospect Hospital on Prospect Ridge, west of the Water Works building. It was an institution where people suffering from tuberculosis (TB) were treated. I did not like making this point. Each time I arrived, a male nurse would say, "Well Officer, we lose one again tonight," referring to the death of a patient.

Afraid of Ghosts

I stayed no longer than necessary after hearing that another patient had died. I cycled as fast as possible to the next point, the residence of the chief justice, because I was afraid of ghosts. From the chief justice's, I visited the receiver general's and treasurer's residences in Highland Park, and then I started back to the station.

On reaching the area between the two golf courses, about two hundred yards from Goodman's Bay, two men jumped out in front of me from behind a cedar tree and shouted in unison, "Hey!" To be honest, I am unable to say exactly what happened after that. But I do know that I broke Jesse Owens' world record for the 100-yard dash because I abandoned my cycle and ran like hell.

While running like hell, and at the same time negotiating my left turn at the junction of Bay Street and Prospect Ridge Road, I heard someone shout, "Burrows!" Then, amidst their laughter, one said, "Come for your cycle. We are [Criminal Investigation Department] (C.I.D.) officers." I was unable to break stride for another fifty feet because of my speed, and it was only then that I slowed my pace and returned. I was met at the corner of Bay Street and Prospect Ridge Road where Detective Constables Calvin Isaacs and Locksley Saunders handed me my cycle. They were both laughing and making fun of me for leaving my cycle and running away.

The CID officers were performing ambush duty, for there was a rapist operating in the area, and had decided to "ambush" me. They were the "good old days," and as members of the Force, we were close to one another, so I took it as a joke and returned to my station.

On my arrival, I reported my beat's happenings to Lance Corporal Wesseling, placing special emphasis on my TOR. I was told to submit my report and to continue with my patrol. I proceeded to area A, the area west of Cable Beach Station, and stopped near the Swank Club.

Shortly after arriving at my point near the club, Sergeant Reginald Deane Dumont, a native of Guyana, visited me. I promptly reported my beat to him. I was also proud to report making my first case that night. Before he left, he encouraged me to continue my good work. That meant much to me, knowing that a sergeant had come out there just to visit me.

Having visited my last point, I returned exhausted to the station at six a.m. After cleaning the station, I was ready to hand it over to the seven a.m. guard. Lance Corporal Joseph Braithwaite, the officer relieving us, informed me that I was to report to the Southern Police Station to await the arrival of Sergeant George Gilbert Moncur. Sergeant Moncur was the station officer at South and was considered the best of all the sergeants. His specialty was drafting charges. He was a "walking penal code" and could draft a charge after the incident was verbally relayed to him. His knowledge of Southern New Providence, indeed the entire island, was sound.

As instructed, I awaited the arrival of Sergeant Moncur, who reported for duty at about seven forty-five a.m. When he arrived, he asked me to accompany him to his office. Once there, he suggested that I give Mr. Austin a break for driving without lights. Mr. Austin, according to Sergeant Moncur, was a friend of the police and would do anything to assist the Force. I learned later, however, that it was Deputy Commissioner Augustus Roberts, with whom Mr. Austin had served in The Bahamas Battalion during World War II, who had initiated the discussion between me and Mr. Moncur.

The next night while patrolling Go Slow Bend, Mr. Austin stopped his truck next to me and said, "Good night, Off-Off-Off-Officer."

"Good night," I said. Then we had a friendly conversation and departed as friends. From that date, we developed a mutual respect for each other. Each time we met thereafter, he called me 303, and I called him MBE.

The Price for Accepting Field Produce

I enjoyed my work at Cable Beach, and with the exception of minor matters coming from Gambier Village, Delaporte, Hobby Horse Hall Racetrack (when in season), the Nassau Beach, Emerald Beach, and Balmoral Beach hotels, the area was quiet.

There were times when I would cycle as far west as Gambier to avoid being bored and to accept the roasted corn, potatoes, and other field products that the residents offered. It was also during this posting that I learned that there wasn't such a thing as a free meal, eventually you would have to pay for it. I paid for that roasted field produce with much humility and embarrassment.

One Saturday while working the two p.m. to ten p.m. shift, I was sent to Nesbitt's Bar in Delaporte to investigate a disturbance. On my arrival, I was surprised to discover that the culprit was one of my Gambier food-producing friends who was drunk and behaving badly. I felt confident that she would listen to me and begin behaving properly. Instead, she continued to be disorderly and began to use some of the most obscene language one could ever imagine. I was reluctant to arrest her, so I tried hard to persuade her to stop. But my efforts proved fruitless. When I told her that she was under arrest, she turned on me and told those gathered how she had given me roasted corn, potatoes, and other produce. The people laughed; I wanted to cry from embarrassment. At the station, she continued her attack. Although several of my colleagues who were also assigned to the Cable Beach Police station were present, they did not react to her comments, for which I was grateful. I was happy when it was eventually all over.

The officers at Cable Beach were Sergeant Reginald Deane Dumont; Lance Corporals Samuel Wesseling and Joseph Braithwaite; Constables Everette Archer, Rudolph Rigby, Wilfred Pinder, Cecil Johnson, Richard Gibbs, and Akel Clarke, who first took me on patrol and showed me the beat.

I got to know other men who made up the Southern Division team, including the men of the Fox Hill and Cable Beach Stations, by attending lectures on Wednesdays. I also got to meet other members of the Force at drill parades at Police Headquarters as periodically all off duty personnel were required to meet there. It was at one of these parades that I got to see the very much talked about, and feared, Inspector Edney Hanlon Johnson and Sergeant Errington Washington Isaac Watkins, alias Bumpy.

Passing Sergeant Watkins

My first encounter with Sergeant Watkins took place some two weeks after seeing him at the drill parade. He was standing just inside the station door at the Southern Police Station, leaning against the counter. I was there waiting to be transported to Cable Beach. I walked past him to exit the station, and he roared, "Boy, what the hell you mean, passing the sergeant without speaking!"

I did not answer because of fear.

"Boy!" he shouted again. "You hear me talking to you?"

I mumbled something to him.

He said, "Get to attention when I speak to you, and don't give me any cheek, before I put you in the 'bloody' cell!"

I stood at attention and was forced to listen to some of the most hurtful things ever said to me. While at training school, Corporal Smith and Lance Corporal McKenzie had said some terrible things, but that was training school.

Before I was allowed to go, Sergeant Watkins wanted to know how I got into the Force. He said that I must have a godfather there, because according to him, I was only five feet tall. I was beginning to think that being short was a crime, and I vowed that at the expiration of my three-year contract, I would leave the Force. This, however, was only the beginning of many such vows. Let me hasten to say that today, Mr. Watkins and I are good friends; also, it was under Sergeant Watkins' command that I received my first promotion.

Needless to say, I tried my best to keep out of the reach of Sergeant Watkins, but that was not possible as he visited Southern Station regularly. Prior to joining the Force, I was only afraid of God. Now I was afraid of God, who promised to send me to hell for failing to keep the commandments, and the sergeant, who had promised to put me in the “bloody” cell for not coming to attention while he spoke. I was beginning to envision hell in the near future and hell in the hereafter.

In those days, Criminal Investigation Department (CID) and Traffic Division both had branches at Central and Southern Stations; they were called CID South and CID Central, Traffic South and Traffic Central. The CID headquarters was located over Central Police Station, and Traffic headquarters was located at West Bay Street in the building formerly used by the beach wardens.

I was working nights for the next two weeks when, at about twelve thirty, I was sent to investigate a traffic accident near the Emerald Beach Hotel. On my arrival, I discovered the accident involved a chief inspector. I saluted the chief inspector and started to investigate. My investigation revealed that he was entering Bay Street from Emerald Beach Hotel’s yard and had collided with the vehicle travelling east on Bay Street.

After the other driver had left the scene, the chief inspector said, “Burrows, don’t let me down.”

I answered, “Yes, sir!” I submitted my report and gave it to the sergeant at the station.

One week later, I reported for duty at two p.m. and was told by Lance Corporal___ that I was to see the chief inspector. I entered his office, and he said, “Burrows, you let me down.”

I responded, “No, sir!”

To this he said, “Yes, sir. Go and see___. He has instructions for you.”

I saluted, left his office, and reported to Lance Corporal___, who sent me back to the chief inspector because, according to him, he did not have any instructions for me. I was sent back for the third time. “Herod” chief inspector and “Pilate” must have gotten their signals crossed that day because the only act missing was the one where they both said, “It was not I who sent you to Special Company, it was he.” ___finally told me that I was not to work that day and that I must report to Special Company, the riot squad, the following morning.

At eight a.m., on February 20, 1962, I reported to the old Army Barracks on Thompson Boulevard, Oakes Field. This site was once used by the British soldiers who came to The Bahamas during the strike of 1958. A number of wooden buildings that made up the complex were given to the police after the British soldiers left The Bahamas. The site of which I write is now that of the new Bahamas Customs building. As I waited with the others to be taken before Deputy Superintendent Leslie Cates, the commanding officer, I wondered what my fate would be in my new surroundings.

The Great Chief Inspector

About fifteen minutes after I reported to the barracks, the others and I were taken before Mr. Cates, a small, thin Englishman with a soft voice. He sent us to see the great Chief Inspector Edney Johnson after he gave us his welcome address. Johnson, a strict disciplinarian, had served as a sergeant in the Bahamas Battalion during the Second World War and had been sent to Jamaica for training.

"Well gad damn! This is a sorry-looking bunch they sent here ay!" were the first words Mr. Johnson said to us. He went to great lengths to explain what he expected of us—we were to do exactly what we were told, how it was told, and when it was told. He continued and said, "I do not want anyone saying 'he thought,' because down here, you don't think—you do. I am the gad damn one down here who thinks, and do not forget that!"

"Yes, sir!" we said. At the lecture's end, we were told that two shillings would be added to our salary, and as a result, much work was expected of us.

Our next stop was Sergeant Eustice "Saco" Turnquest's office. Turnquest could relate to any situation and got along with both superiors and juniors. I thoroughly enjoyed working with Turnquest, for he had a great sense of humour and could see the funny side in any situation.

Sitting next to Turnquest in his office was another sergeant, Eric Hepburn. I must admit that Sergeant Hepburn was a man whom I never understood. His famous words were, "Don't argue with me. I am the troop sergeant. Look at all that knoxin on your belt." Unlike Turnquest, Hepburn saw the worst in every situation.

The Special Company Division was divided into three troops: A, B, and C. Troop A was under the command of Chief Inspector Edney Johnson; troop B, Errington Watkins; and troop C was the police band. I was sent to troop A, where Edney Johnson was waiting for me.

After collecting our accoutrements, which consisted of a wicker shield, baton, tear gas, mask, and other items, we were herded into a lecture room and briefed on our assignments. We operated by the sound of a loud whistle, which Sergeant Hepburn enjoyed using. He would close his eyes and turn that thing on, looking periodically at his watch to see how long it would take all of us to fall in. Whatever we were doing, we were expected to drop it when the whistle blew, grab our batons and shields, and fall in line at the front of the office block.

Early the following morning, Sergeant Turnquest took us onto the Oakes Field runway near the old hangar for rifle drills. We were practicing for the opening of the Supreme Court, and Mr. Edney Johnson was to join Sergeant Turnquest at eight thirty.

Only a Little Sweat Left

On Johnson's arrival, Turnquest called the parade to attention and took us through a few drills. Then Johnson suddenly growled, "Take the bayonets off the rifle and high port [which means place the rifle over your head with both hands]." His next order was, "Double march!" Edney Johnson ran us up and down the runway until very little sweat was left in our bodies. He then snarled, "The next time you come on my parade drilling in a sloppy manner, I will run you until your tongues look like neckties hanging from your mouths."

At ten a.m., we were taken to various points on Wulff Road, East Street, Nassau Street, and Baillou Hill Road to perform traffic duties. This lasted until about two. Then meals were served when we arrived at Oakes Field.

A general election was scheduled to take place during November 1962. As a result, Special Company was training day and night. Even in my sleep I could hear, "Advance! Return!" and the sound of tear gas shells hitting the ground. We had very little time off, and whenever we complained, we were reminded of the two shillings we were receiving for being in Special Company. I often wished that they would take the money back and allow me to work sensible hours.

In the course of a day, we were expected to perform any of the following: Hobby Horse Hall Racetrack, for general police duties, traffic duty, guard duty at Main Guard at Police Headquarters and Government House, road blocks, political meetings, and riot and rifle drills.

As the general election neared, political meetings were held more frequently and, at times, carried on late into the night.

Much was said about this election because this was the first time that women would be allowed to vote, and it was felt that the Progressive Liberal Party would be victorious at the polls. I vividly remember Mr. Henry Milton Taylor, of the Progressive Liberal Party, and Mr. Lynden Pindling speaking at the meetings. When I was not working at political meetings, I was required to "stand to" at Oakes Field with my riot shield and baton nearby.

I disliked working at Hobby Horse Hall for a number of reasons; one being the shabby treatment that we received. When it was time to eat, sergeants, corporals, and constables were given dried peas and rice and a small piece of mutilated chicken served in a snack box. The building in which we were housed was too small, and we ate at different times. After we complained, and we did so frequently, the racetrack's owner ordered an apple thrown into our snack boxes for good measure. For it was the owner of the track's responsibility to feed us. On one occasion, an inspector told us that the track owner was doing us a favor and that we should not complain. You see, the inspector ate in the restaurant with the other officials.

Sergeant McFerris Orlando Hanna promised that if and when he became inspector, he would see to it that we ate in the restaurant. During the next promotion exercise, Hanna was made an acting inspector and was given Hobby Horse Hall restaurant status. After two track meets, we were still dining on that not so sumptuous meal. I approached Hanna and reminded him of his promise. He said that his hour had not yet come, and that he would make his move when he had been confirmed to a full inspector. I thought that was reasonable and waited in anticipation for his confirmation to full inspector.

Six months later, Hanna's promotion to inspector was announced, and the other snack box eaters and I were happy. The happiness, however, was short-lived. When I reminded Hanna of his promise, he said, "Burrows, you just joined this job, and it will take you some time yet before you really understand what it is all about. If you work hard, then one day you too will be an inspector, and then you will be able to eat in the clubhouse restaurant." Change however did come and before I left the Special Company, all ranks were allowed to eat in the Hobby Horse Hall Racetrack restaurant. No thanks, of course, to Hanna.

In Special Company, we were treated as though we were in the army. The officers and sub-officers ran races to charge us with the most stupid things. Many officers, I thought, were unfairly treated and dismissed for trivial matters.

I was at a disadvantage in the Company because I had no home or place to go to. I stayed around the compound most of the time because my aunt's and uncle's treatment had caused me to lose faith in human beings. When a Guard was short due to persons reporting sick, I was often detailed to fill in particularly at Government House or the Main Guard even though I might have just completed a tour of duty. During this period, I was unhappy and prayed for the expiration of my three-year contract. There were times when I cried bitterly and longed to be in Matthew Town, Inagua, with my family. I even approached Mr. Johnson and requested to be sent home, but to no avail. He said that they had sent for my father, but I had come instead, which was an old army saying.

Prior to Election Day, I was involved in a serious traffic accident. I had spoken with Constable Peter McLean Cox, who always seemed to have the answer to every question, about having to work whenever the Guards were short. He suggested that I join him at his aunt's place, the Fiesta, whenever I was off duty. The Fiesta was a restaurant and bar on Poinciana Drive near Hospital Lane. His relatives actually resided on Hospital Lane, and I would usually stop there before going to the bar.

One Saturday night, I left my place of residence in a slight drizzle to meet with my friend Cox (and to avoid being detailed to work should a constable report in sick). I was hungry, so I decided to purchase a chicken-in-the-bag and a soda from the Reef Restaurant. I set off on my cycle and made my purchase with the intent of eating it at my friend's home.

As I left the Reef Restaurant, the drizzle turned into heavy rain. Some hours later, I opened my eyes in the Princess Margaret Hospital. The doctor told me that I was lucky to be alive, as I could have been killed. I had been struck from behind by a police patrol car driven by Constable Frederick Russell, and with him was Sergeant Alphonso Marshall.

Recollection of my Experiences along Life's Convoluted Path

"Frederick Russell," the magistrate shouted, "how do you plead?"

"Not guilty," Russell replied.

After a week's adjournment at the courts, Russell maintained his not guilty plea. On completing my testimony, and once Sergeant Alphonso Marshall completed his, Russell took the witness stand.

"On the date in question," Russell said, "while driving a patrol car accompanied by Sergeant Marshall, travelling north on Thompson Boulevard at ten miles per hour and in heavy rain, I became blinded by the bright lights of an oncoming car. Shortly thereafter, I heard a sound and saw a man flying through the air, finally landing on the patrol car hood. The man, I thought, was knocked crazy because he was holding tightly on to a bottle of soda and was in a frenzy trying to recover a lost object, which turned out to be a chicken-in-the-bag."

Russell ended his evidence by telling the court that I was taken to the hospital only after being allowed to eat my provisions. Sergeant Cyril Joseph, the able prosecutor, on cross-examination asked Russell why he continued to drive after he was blinded by the lights of an oncoming car. To this, he did not reply. He was found guilty and cautioned.

As a result of the accident, I sustained a deep wound to my back, facial injuries, and lacerations to my legs. My cycle and clothing were also destroyed. At the hospital I was detained for observation and released the following morning with fourteen days to nurse my wounds. At my quarters, I was cared for by my colleagues whenever they were available. I was happy to return to my duties and to resume my normal life.

On my return, Chief Inspector Edney Johnson remarked, "Well gad damn! Boy, they still gat you round here?" Then he said, "Anyhow, for two whole damn weeks you draw government money on slack. Now back in the lineup. That means you work twice as hard to make up for that slack money you did not work for."

"Yes, sir," I said.

Shortly after my encounter with Mr. Johnson, I ran into Inspector Watkins. He asked me if I was still skimping, and he said that I was holding up the practice parade for the visit of President John F. Kennedy of the United States, Prime Minister John Diefenbaker of Canada, and Prime Minister Harold MacMillan of Great Britain. The men of the Special Company who formed the guard of honour spent many hard days practicing for the occasion. We were relieved when it was all over.

A New Era

After occasions like that one, parading for visiting dignitaries, we were entertained with drinks at the Canteen at Oakes Field courtesy of our superiors. It was also the beginning of a new era for me with regard to my lifestyle. While at the Canteen, Constable Ralph Butler invited me to visit with him at his aunt's house and place of business on Second Street, Coconut Grove. Without hesitation, I accepted his offer. A few hours later, I found myself sipping Beck's beer from a bottle, while comfortably seated at the home of Mrs. Rowena Deveaux.

As the hours passed, I was introduced to other family members. Among them was a young, beautiful girl with large eyes named Dorothy McKinney. By this time, I had consumed four bottles of beer and therefore wanted to put in my application for favourable consideration, but I decided instead to use my head and not my heart. It would have been foolish, I thought, to wear out my welcome on the first visit to the home of a friend's relative. Prior to Ralph and me making our exit, Ralph's uncle, Vincent Walkes, treated us to bowls of delicious sheep tongue souse.

The following Saturday, Ralph invited me to go with him again to visit his aunt, and I graciously went along. As before, I was wined, dined, and made to feel at home. The visit, however, was not complete until my eyes beheld the beauty of Dorothy. The chocolate-brown, full-eyed darling entered the gate to pay her respects to her grandmother. I determined to get to know this darling better. So feeling in top spirits from the beers, I commenced my line of questioning.

"Where do you live?"

"At Fifth Street Coconut Grove," she replied.

"Which school do you attend?"

"Western Senior," she said.

The ice being broken thus far, I left with Ralph for our residences feeling proud. Before exiting Ralph's car, I told him of my admiration for his cousin and asked him to take me along whenever the occasion arose. This, however, did not happen often because Ralph was in troop B and I was in troop A. Whenever I was on duty; he was off and vice versa. "Where there is a will, there is a way," I remember my father saying to my mother.

At the thought of my father's words, I approached Mr. Watkins with the idea of being transferred to his section. I must have approached him at the wrong time, however, because as the old folks say, "The only thing that I was not told was that I was a child of God."

He said, "You gad damn, tied-tongue, far-island, barefoot fella should be glad you have a job, and now you talking 'bout where you want to work!" As if that wasn't enough, he marched me before Edney Johnson and told him, "Edney, this damn boy said he don't want to work with you. I bring him so you could deal with him."

I was afraid and thought that I was on my way to being fired, but this did not happen.

New Found Interest

I was very surprised when Mr. Johnson enquired my reason for wanting a transfer. I was candid with him and said that Ralph Butler was a close friend and that I had no other friend or family in New Providence on whom I could rely and feel comfortable with. I went on to explain my new place of interest and that Ralph had a car and I did not even have a bicycle. This was the first time that I saw Mr. Johnson smile. Prior to this, if it was not the law of nature that a man must yawn, I would not have known that Mr. Johnson had teeth.

After much discussion, I left Mr. Johnson's office with his words, "Go. We will see what will happen." I was not optimistic at all when I left his office.

Two days later, I was invited to Mr. Watkins's office. Chief Inspector Johnson and Sergeant Turnquest were waiting there, too. Mr. Watkins informed me that I was being given the job of supervising uniformed prisoners and serving tea, among other things, to the office staff. Then Mr. Johnson asked me if I could make tea, to which I hurriedly answered, "Extremely well, sir!"

The next day at seven a.m., I left Oakes Field in a Land Rover to collect prisoners from H. M. Prison. We collected Mr. Johnson from his residence on Plantol Street on our way back from the prison. I enjoyed my new assignment very much. My visits to Second Street became more frequent; I was beginning to enjoy Nassau.

November 19, the anniversary of Dorothy's birth, was approaching. A party was to be held in her honour, and I was invited. I awaited the nineteenth with anticipation and was among the first to arrive at the party's venue.

I ordered a rum and coke from the bartender who, coincidentally, was Dorothy's brother Andrew McKinney. The first drink, I am sure, was Bacardi and coke. The others I am not certain, because half an hour later, after my third drink, I was unsteady on my feet and my speech was slurred.

Although I was feeling sick, I stayed to the party's end so that I could escort Dorothy home. I was drunk and staggered often on her tiny feet. Before I departed her home, I told her of my feelings for her, and she replied with her usual, "I don't know."

The following day, I felt as though the weight of the world was on my head. I was sick for several days and vowed that I would never take another drop of liquor.

I visited Dorothy regularly after the party, having been granted visiting rights by her mother. Some months later, my friend Ralph informed that Andrew had mixed about six different brands of liquor each time I had requested a drink at Dorothy's party. It was wicked of a young man attending Queen's College.

Having to travel between Coconut Grove and my residence was causing a problem, so I endeavoured to recoup my cycle. As a result of my plight, I spoke with Sergeant Keith Mason, who had recently arrived on transfer from Abaco. Sergeant Mason sent me to consult with Mr. Paul Adderley, a barrister-at-law, with respect to the court having my cycle replaced.

Mr. Adderley advised me not to pursue the idea of suing the Police Force for the restoration of my cycle. He promised, instead, to speak with the acting deputy commissioner, Major Wenzel V. Granger. The acting deputy commissioner agreed to give me fifteen pounds to defray the expenses of my cycle and clothing. On short order, I replaced my cycle and bought new clothing to replace those damaged in the accident.

I was now making frequent trips to the Grove to see the pride and joy of my life—Dorothy. Finding a girlfriend brought a new dimension to my life, or so it seemed. Both Mr. Watkins and Mr. Johnson began to ease up on me a little too. They told me not to take them or their uncomplimentary remarks seriously, but to laugh instead. So I did.

Constantly Under Attack

The attention that was once focused on me was passed on to a young man from Crooked Island, Reginald Farquharson. According to Watkins, soap and water were Farquharson's enemies. There were many days when I comforted and encouraged him not to quit the Force. Constable Irwin Seymour, alias Dusty, was also constantly under attack. Mr. Watkins would tell Seymour how ugly he thought he was, and Seymour would reply that God made him in his (God's) image. Then Watkins would say, "Boy, stop lying, because God don't make mistakes."

During the first week of December, 1962, I was detailed to make a cup of tea for a gentleman. Chief Inspector Johnson informed me that I made the worst cup of tea he had ever drunk. At this, the recipient of the tea laughed and asked me my name and job description. Mr. Johnson informed him that OJ (odd jobs) was my job description.

Mr. Johnson's guest asked me if I would like to work at Police Headquarters.

"Doing what?" I asked.

"Working in the Pay Office."

I said, "Yes, sir. I would enjoy that very much."

Then he informed me that his name was Leifred Walton Johnson, chief inspector and paymaster of the Police Force. Mr. Leifred Johnson was travelling to the United States to purchase an automobile and promised that upon his return he would contact me.

By working around the compound and office, I was always in contact with the authorities, and as a result, I got to know their likes and dislikes. Deputy Superintendent Leslie Cates, the officer-in-charge of the Special Company, was kind to me, and so was Deputy Superintendent Dennis Morgan, the police band's director.

Members of the Progressive Liberal Party took the loss of the 1962 general election hard, and that was the talk around town at the year's end. The Police's annual Christmas dinner was cancelled and everything during December 1962, was low-keyed, except of course at my place of employment. Wherever Edney Johnson and Errington Watkins were, nothing in their vicinity could be termed "quiet."

Unlike the previous Christmas, I was very happy in the company of my new-found love for nothing else can be a substitute for happiness. I spent my time off duty at the McKinney's residence, and as far as I was concerned, the rest of the world did not exist. Chief Inspector Leifred Johnson came through on his promise to have me work with him at Police Headquarters on January 4, 1963.

When I was summoned to Police Headquarters to see the commissioner of police, Edward Colchester-Wemyss, Mr. Cates told me to refuse the transfer and remain at Special Company, if I were given the choice. However, I harboured no such thought, and when I arrived at the "Lion's" door, ("Lion" was the commissioner's radio call sign) saying yes to the transfer was indelibly etched into my mind.

I was looking forward to leaving the Special Company for two reasons: (1) to get away from Edney Johnson, Errington Watkins, and Eric Hepburn; and (2) for a change in my job description. I yearned for a transfer to a place where men were treated with respect and dignity.

"Not Headquarters Material"

My first day at Headquarters was not pleasant. Mr. Leifred Johnson, the paymaster, introduced me to the staff, the first being Mr. Wenzel Granger, who also hailed from Inagua. Mr. Johnson said, "Mr. Granger, this is Constable 303 Burrows, the replacement for Constable 323 Moss at the Dispatch and Records Office. He is also your homeboy from Inagua."

All seemed to be going well with Mr. Johnson's introduction—until he got to the "homeboy" part. On hearing it, Mr. Granger took out the pipe he was biting on and grunted, "What gad damn homeboy? You see me have any homeboy looking like him? His hair needs cutting, his trousers are filthy, his tunic is too small, he did not shave this morning, and his boots are not clean. You better take him out of here quick, before the commissioner sees him, and he is kicked out of the gate." To this, my escort saluted and escorted me to his office where I was sent away to smarten up.

On my return, Mr. Johnson took me back to see Mr. Granger. And again, he said with a grunt, "Leifred, it would appear as though he wants to work at Headquarters. Why the hell you did not shave this morning?"

"Sir, I did shave this morning," I replied.

He shouted, "Are you calling the deputy commissioner a liar?"

"No, sir," I said, "I shaved this morning."

Mr. Granger grunted again and said, "Then in future, stand closer to your razor blade."

"Yes, sir."

I was then taken to the commissioner's office where I met for the first time the very much talked about Commissioner Colchester-Wemyss.

This time Mr. Granger did the introductions. He said, "Commissioner, I don't know what you think of him, but this is who Leifred brought to Headquarters. He doesn't look like Headquarters material to me, but I brought him for you to see."

To this, the commissioner replied, "Laddie, who the hell let you through the gate?"

I did not answer.

After making other uncomplimentary remarks about my height, the commissioner informed me that I was to be kept at Headquarters on a month's trial, and if I failed to measure up to expectation, I was to be sent to the Fire Branch. The Fire Branch, at that time, was considered a place for human rejects. Before being dismissed, Mr. Granger said that I was to be watched closely.

I thanked Mr. Leifred Johnson for trying to help me by having me on his staff and further commented that if my stay at Headquarters would be in accordance with my introduction, then it was better that I return from whence I came. Mr. Johnson smiled and said, "You are not going a step. You will work in Headquarters and make a man of yourself. In there, they are only trying to scare you, but you will soon see that they are not all that bad." Then he took me to see Mr. Noel Thompson, the staff officer, who in turn took me back to the Records Office.

Records and Dispatch Office

I was posted to the Records and Dispatch Office at Police Headquarters, where I met Corporal Earl Alleyne and Constable Sherman Rigby. Alleyne and Rigby were typists and clerical assistants to the commissioner's office. Assistant Superintendent Noel Thompson was the staff officer; Major Wenzel Granger, whom everyone feared, was the acting deputy commissioner; and Lieutenant-Colonel E. J. H. Colchester-Wemyss, alias Lion, was the commissioner.

The Pay Office consisted of Chief Inspector Leifred Johnson, paymaster; Corporal Alonzo Butler; Lance Corporal Kenneth Saunders; Lance Corporal Errol Farquharson; and Constable Ortland Fynes. In the Police Stores were Corporal Ivan Brooks and Lance Corporal Bernard Turner.

The following day, I reported for duty at eight a.m. as instructed. Constable Rigby came shortly thereafter and introduced me to a mop and bucket filled with water. Then he took me to the commissioner's office where I fatigued the pay officer's, staff officer's, and deputy commissioner's offices and then, very carefully, the commissioner's office. My next chore was to sharpen all the pencils, change the blotting papers, fill the ink wells, and, finally, clean all the wastepaper baskets. At eight forty-five a.m., the other staff members began arriving; the commissioner arrived at about nine.

Large Delivery Box

Next, Constable Rigby took me to see the staff officer. He asked him whether there was any urgent dispatch for Government House or the colonial secretary's office. The staff officer answered yes to both and gave me a large blue box with the letters "BP" (Bahamas Police) written in red with the documents for delivery. With Constable Rigby bearing a brown leather bag, we left Headquarters on foot. Our first stop was Government House where we left letters from the box. Next we visited the office of the colonial secretary where we deposited and collected more letters. Our next stops were made in the following order: the Public Board of Works at Nassau Court; the Public Treasury at the corner of Shirley Street and School Lane; the General Post Office on Bank Lane; and then downstairs in the Senate building, where Constable Rigby filled his bag with mail.

My tunic was soaked and I was exhausted when I returned to Headquarters. Constable Rigby then explained the method for sorting and distributing the letters for members of the Force. Halfway through this process, I was called to the Pay Office where I was given urgent mail for the Treasury, Government House, and the Public Board of Works. This time I was given a bicycle and was told to make it quick, because the pay sheet that was being prepared had to be delivered to the Treasury before eleven a.m. I did as I was instructed, only to be sent back to the Treasury immediately after reentering Headquarters. Then from the Treasury, I was sent to the Canteen to purchase sodas and biscuits for my seniors. I was given one chore after another to perform. At the end of the day, I was happy to retire. The following morning, I did the same chores over again that I had done the day before. This time, however, Constable Rigby was missing.

I performed my given tasks with distinction during the next four months. I dared not question the authorities for fear of being sent to Fire Branch, but I thought that it was unfair that both Rigby and I were constables yet I had to make all the rounds. I tried my best to keep out of the way of both the commissioner and his deputy. This was difficult, though, because I was often sent on errands for Mr. Granger.

Records and Dispatch Office—Again

I won the confidence of those in authority as time passed. However, I remained afraid of the deputy, who never smiled. I was therefore surprised one morning while cleaning his office; he came in early, and he was in a good mood. He said, "Constable, you will be pleased to learn that I had the wrong concept of you. The COP [commissioner of police] thinks you are a good lad, and so do I. Don't let that go to your damn head, though."

Realizing that I was now in the good graces of the powers that be, and with the workload ever increasing, I petitioned Corporal Alleyne for additional help. I informed him that I thought that Rigby should alternate with me and do some of the chores as we were both constables. Alleyne did not accept this and said that Rigby was senior to me and a typist. Not satisfied with Alleyne's answer, I complained to Mr. Noel Thompson, the impressive-looking, good-natured staff officer. I told Mr. Thompson that while it was true that I had left school at an early age, and that I had left the same way in which I had entered, without certificates, I had learned, while there, that slavery had been abolished. I feared that that bit of information had not yet reached the capital of Nassau or, if it had, the Police Force was not yet the benefactor of that piece of English legislation because of the amount of work that I was required to do. Mr. Thompson readily agreed with my comments and promised to ease my plight.

The next day, I was instructed to take the assigned bicycle to the police garage, where it was to be fitted with a large basket. I was told to collect it the following morning, and I did. On my return, the commissioner, his deputy, the staff officer, and Corporal Alleyne came to watch a display of my ability to ride a bicycle with an oversized basket bearing a box and a bag of letters and parcels.

The commissioner instructed me to mount the contraption. No sooner had I complied, and then I found myself and the cycle on the hood of the deputy's car. The oversized basket was too large and heavy for the cycle, which made balancing difficult. (Let me hastily add that I did very little to control the cycle, for it would have been embarrassing to be seen around town on that machine.)

Mr. Granger said, "The damn man wants to mash up my car right here in Barracks. We better take the basket off before he kills himself in traffic out there on the streets." The commissioner then instructed that a motorcyclist be assigned to Headquarters to take me on my rounds.

Assistance with Delivery

The next morning, Constable Saunders arrived at Headquarters from Traffic to assist me with deliveries. He was a good and efficient officer whom I found to be honest in all his dealings. Unfortunately, this fine young man was killed by an ambulance at the junction of Market Street and Wulff Road sometime later. He was replaced by Constable Charles Arthur Stewart.

This officer was a policeman at heart, but his power of reasoning was poor. There was, according to him, only one way of doing things—Stewart's way. He would often ride his motorcycle just under the speed limit for a given area, and he would stop any motorist who passed him. Then he would either book the motorist or let him or her off with a sound scolding. We were friends, but his method of doing things did not coincide with mine.

When the time came for Constable Stewart and the Force to part company, he was relieved by Constable Jerome Bethell. Constable Bethell was a sensible officer who was calm and collected at all times, nothing could ruffle his composure. He was pleasant and thorough. Constable Bethel later joined the Road Traffic Department. The Force's loss, however, was that Department's gain.

During the summer of 1963, I was granted three weeks vacation leave. So I visited my native Inagua, and this time, I was able to afford a ticket on Bahamas Airways. The duration of my leave was spent with my family, with the exception of my sister Miriam and my brother Aiden, who had both left prior to my leaving. Aiden was a lighthouse keeper at Bird Rock, and

Miriam was on a Family Island where she performed domestic duties for a commissioner.

On my return to Nassau, I resumed my steady visits with Dorothy and enjoyed every minute of them. We were now going steady and our relationship was beginning to blossom.

The year 1961 was full of excitement in the life of the Force. During May 1962 a commission of inquiry was appointed to inquire into alleged misconduct by the commissioner of police, Mr. Colchester-Wemyss. I had the good fortune of working at the inquiry, which was held at Carlton House, East Street. Suffice it to say, the commissioner's stay in the Force was shortened at the inquiry's end, for he parted company with the Force he had done so much for on April 22, 1963. With the departure of the commissioner, Mr. Granger, the deputy commissioner, was appointed acting commissioner, and Mr. George C. Lavell was appointed acting deputy commissioner.

New Commissioner Arrives

The acting appointment of both officers lasted until July 29, 1963, for on the twenty-ninth, ex-deputy inspector general, Mr. Nigel Godfrey Morris, arrived from the United Kingdom and assumed duties as the commissioner of police. Mr. Morris, who was nearing fifty-five years of age at the time of his appointment, was an able administrator. Among some of the first changes he made was to abolish the short trousers worn by inspectors and senior officers to long trousers and a scarf. The scarf, of course, was optional.

It was also interesting to know that Mr. Morris's predecessor received a salary of £2,225 per annum, while Mr. Morris received twice as much.

Mr. Roy Solomon, the member of Parliament for Rum Cay and San Salvador at the time, was considered the unofficial "minister of police." This, of course, was before ministerial government; it was not until 1964 that The Bahamas was granted full internal self-government. The talks for the new Constitution, however, were held in London during 1963.

The black population of The Bahamas was disappointed that Uncle Wenzel, as Mr. Granger was called behind his back, was not made commissioner. His stay in the Force lasted until July 1, 1964, at which time he was promoted and transferred to the Immigration Department as chief immigration officer, a title that was later changed to director of immigration.

Mr. Granger, who later owned me as his homeboy, was born in 1909. He had seen military service with the Bahamas Battalion from 1942 to 1946. He served in Italy and Egypt and was demobilized at the rank of captain. In October 1946, he was appointed inspector of police in the Royal Bahamas

Police Force. On November 6, 1951, he was promoted to assistant superintendent of police, and on July 1, 1955, he was transferred to the Out Island Department as commissioner.

In December 1958 he returned to the Force and was promoted to superintendent of police in May 1959. He became deputy commissioner of police during 1962.

On October 1, 1969, Mr. Granger was again appointed to the post of administrative officer (auxiliaries) in the Royal Bahamas Police Force. He held that position for just thirteen months.

The Perfect Gentleman

Mr. Granger was considered the perfect gentleman in the Police Force. He had a sterling character and displayed personal and professional qualities at all times. He also had extremely poor handwriting. When Mr. Granger was shown his handwriting a few days after he wrote it, even he had difficulty understanding it.

He also had a dry sense of humor. Inspector Samuel Davis told me of an incident that reportedly happened one Saturday night how while being taken on an inspection tour of the city, Mr. Granger, on arriving at Prince George Dock, observed four prostitutes sitting on a bench. He approached the women and inquired their reasons for being there. They informed him that they were fishing. To this, Mr. Granger replied, "If you are fishing, you must be sitting on your damn bait."

Once, Mr. Granger sent me to Lowe's Pharmacy on Bay Street to purchase one extra-hard bristled Tek toothbrush, but the clerk gave me a toothbrush minus the Tek. He asked me to return it and obtain the correct toothbrush. After making three trips to the pharmacy, and being given one toothbrush after another that was missing one of the requirements, Mr. Granger finally said, "Burrows, we must then await the arrival of the perfect brush."

I shall always remember December 1963, for it was the month Dorothy and I commenced making plans for matrimony. We both desired a February wedding, but being Anglicans, we were forbidden because of the Lenten season. Father John Calnan, rector of Saint Barnabas Church, agreed to perform the ceremony on April 15, 1964, instead. With the grand sum of fifteen pounds in the bank and the promise of an asue draw of one hundred and fifty pounds, I committed to take unto myself a wife.

Love, as we all know, is blind and knows no barriers, so I continued making the necessary preparations despite the letter my father sent me. He had ended his letter with the following: "Son, there are three things a man should endeavor to shun in his life if he is to be successful: (a) a bad woman, (b) having to eat bad food, and (c) a bad running car." He also said that a combination of any of the aforementioned is a sure passport to early eternity.

Cabinet Deliveries

On January 7, 1964, The Bahamas Constitution changed from being a colony of Great Britain to that of internal self-government. Britain was now only responsible for external affairs in matters pertaining to The Bahamas and its defence. With the Constitution's change, a Premier and Cabinet were appointed to replace the Executive Council. The Cabinet consisted of sixteen members, which included the Premier.

On the formation of the Cabinet, I was detailed, along with Constable Clebert Deleveaux, to deliver, when necessary, special documents in briefcases to the Ministers of Cabinet. I did the delivery, while Constable Deleveaux chauffeured me to the various ministers' addresses. I recall my first delivery very well. I was instructed, before leaving the Cabinet Office, to deliver the briefcases to the ministers only, and if they were not at their offices or homes, I was to return the cases to the Cabinet Office or, after the closure of Cabinet, to the police control room. Public offices, in 1964, were opened till noon on Saturdays and nine a.m. to five p.m. on regular workdays.

As instructed, I left Cabinet with the briefcases and decided to walk to Solomon's Mines on Bay Street, where I met the Minister for Post and Telecommunications, the Honourable Roy M. Solomon, who gladly signed my receipt book. Then I went to the office of the Honourable Stafford L. Sands, Minister of Tourism and Finance. A white gentleman greeted me at Mr. Sands's office and inquired of my presence. I informed him that I wished to speak with and deliver to Mr. Sands the briefcase in my hand. To this, and in amazement, the man replied, "Who ass told you to say that? They know you could never see the Minister." I told him that if I did not see the Minister and obtain his signature, I would have to return the briefcase to Cabinet. To that, he replied, "Then you will be taking that back all the time, because you will never see the Minister."

So I took the briefcase back to Cabinet and informed a clerk there of my encounter at Minister Sands' office, only to be told that clearance had been given to leave the finance minister's briefcase with Mr. X, the white man I had encountered.

On my return to the aforementioned address, Mr. X said, "Officer, how long have you been on the Force? You have plenty to learn around here." Embarrassed, I had Mr. X sign my book. Then I left bewildered. The episode taught me that there are times when one must endure the unendurable and suffer the insufferable.

Deleveaux and I performed Cabinet duties for quite some time. And on Saturdays, after deliveries, we would go to the Police Canteen at Police Headquarters and feast on beers and salty sausages with biscuits. Deleveaux was a likeable chap, but after consuming two beers, he would start speaking in "tongues." Some of the officers, however, called it Spanish. I once asked an officer how he knew that Deleveaux was speaking Spanish when he did not understand Spanish himself. The officer concurred with my "original" thought.

Top Row: Edward Colchester-Wemyss, Nigel Morris
Middle Row: Thomas Clunie, John Hindmarsh
Bottom Row: Wenzel Granger, Albert Miller

Wedding Bells

As time drew nearer to the wedding, Dorothy and I visited a number of furniture stores in search of bargains. We finally decided to do business with Central Furniture on Bay Street. After making our furniture selection and the usual one-third deposit the saleswoman, she then sent me to Commonwealth Industrial Bank to arrange financing.

I was shown to a cubicle in the bank and was asked to await the arrival of a loan officer. After waiting for what seemed like an hour, a man finally appeared with his hands full of papers. It was another full hour, after an intense discussion, before he finally said, "I will see you in a week's time."

The loan officer who conducted that meeting must have worked for the KGB, for the only question that he omitted to ask was the time that I was to die at. I would highly recommend him for a position on the Royal Bahamas Police Force.

The following day, I visited with Dorothy, only to have her mother ask me if I had given her name as a reference at a bank. I said yes. Mr. Leifred Johnson, the Force paymaster, was also called as a reference for my loan request.

On my return to the bank a week later, the loan officer told me that my mother-in-law-to-be had to sign the loan as guarantor because I was not yet twenty-one. I thought this to be a poor start on my ability to support a wife, but I agreed to Marjorie, my mother-in-law-to-be, signing for the furniture. The loan officer also told me that the down payment was not sufficient to include a refrigerator. So I had to purchase a third-hand one from Besco's Furniture Store on Dowdeswell Street. It was the first refrigerator that I had seen that required a padlock and key to open and shut it.

It was now time to select wedding garments, and Dorothy thought I would look smart in a tuxedo. I was pleased to inform her of the black tuxedo, shoes, shirt, and other necessary articles that I had divested my uncle of, since he had earlier relieved me of my cash through fraudulent means. On inspection of the clothing I had appropriated, however, the only thing she was in agreement with was a pair of black socks. I was forced to dump the rest.

Two days later, I received a telephone call informing me that the furniture was ready for delivery. I asked that it be held until a house was secured to place it in. This was a clear case of placing the cart in front of the horse.

As fate would have it, that same afternoon my soon-to-be-in-laws offered me and Dorothy the use of a four-room house they owned on Second Street, Coconut Grove. The tenants were served notice to vacate the premises, and I proceeded to put the house in order for habitation. The outside toilet needed major repairs, so I hired a carpenter to make them.

With everything in place, the fifteenth of April fast approaching, and no wedding suit or money to purchase one, I petitioned Mr. Rubin Bott, the owner of Rubin's Department Store on George Street, for help. I had come to know Rubin from his frequenting Police Headquarters on official business, in which I often assisted. Having apprised the good gentleman of my situation, he rose responsive to my cry, and in short order, he had outfitted me from neck to toe. He requested a down payment, but because of my financial embarrassment, I was allowed to leave the store with the merchandise.

A week prior to the occasion, my parents sent one of my brothers from Inagua to represent the family. He came bearing a letter, one quart of lima beans, and ten pounds of good old Inagua wild hog meat. The letter, in part, stated: "Son, as you know, we are poor people and Inagua is far. The family sends their love, take care of yourself, and God be with you."

With those words of comfort foremost in my mind at four p.m. on April 15, 1964, at Saint Barnabas Anglican Church, I solemnly declared, "I know not of any impediment why I, Rodney Ador Burrows, should not be joined in holy matrimony to Dorothy Eloise McKinney."

The wedding ceremony thus ended, the bridal party assembled at the residence of Dorothy's grandmother, Mrs. Rowena Deveaux at Second Street, Coconut Grove, for the commencement of the wedding feast.

At both venues, church and reception, the majority of the guests gathered were Dorothy's invitees. This was also the case in respect to the gifts we received. The few guests that I had invited only attended the reception.

The photography of the entire wedding ceremony was disastrous. My new in-laws had secured the services of a friend to photograph the proceedings. And the only thing that the photographer did right was to show up at the right places where the events were held.

We were disappointed with the photographer's finished product. There were photos showing either heads and no feet or feet without heads. Those that came out fairly well had Dorothy's eyes half or completely closed. For us allowing him to improve his proficiency in photography, he relieved me of five pounds.

After the reception ended, Dorothy and I were driven by her cousin Ralph in a blue Ford Consul number 1313 to our new home where we began a week's honeymoon. The next morning, I had to perform the painful task of a water boy as the house did not have inside plumbing. With two brand new buckets in hand, I reluctantly walked to the faucet at the end of the corner where a queue for water had formed.

As a boy in Inagua, I had performed the task of toting water; however, I had since gotten used to the comfort and luxury found in modern facilities since joining the force and now it was back to the basics of life. My in-laws, who lived close by, regularly provided meals, and for recreation, we would walk from our address to theirs. There were also times when we walked to and from the Capitol Theatre to view films.

My week's leave having expired, I returned to work somewhat lame from what I term the "honeymoon blues."

Mr. Granger, the deputy commissioner of police, on seeing me said, "What the hell, I heard you went like a damn fool and got married."

"Yes, sir," I replied.

"And why the hell you did not let me know?"

I did not answer.

"Where is your wife from?" he asked.

"Nassau," I said.

"Where is she employed?"

"She was a student before marriage," I answered.

"Why did you marry someone who is not employed?"

"Because I love her," was my answer.

"Then why the hell you did not find someone who was working to love?"

That question I refused to answer.

He dismissed me with the words, "Come and see me at three p.m."

I returned to his office as instructed at three p.m. To my surprise, Mr. Granger handed me an envelope while saying, "This is your present. Take care of your wife and don't be like some of these worthless policemen around here, drinking plenty of liquor, keeping plenty sweethearts, and don't go home to their wives." I thanked him most sincerely and left his office with his gift, which turned out to be a card and a five pound note. As I mentioned earlier, "Uncle Wenzel" Granger was a strange man with equally strange ways.

My weekly income in 1964 was twelve pounds (thirty-six dollars), plus a housing allowance of seven pounds (twenty-one dollars) per month. Dorothy, a student prior to our marriage, was unemployed, which meant that things were tough.

I was required to pay twelve pounds per month to the Commonwealth Industrial Bank, two pounds per week to Rubin's Department Store, five pounds per week went to an asue, and the remainder went to groceries. When the end of the month came to pay the bank for the furniture, I was forced to seek assistance from my stepfather, Mr. Leifred Johnson (I refer to him as "stepfather" because of what the good gentleman did for me and my wife during those difficult days). I seemed to be coping well on my meager income, at first, but as time went on, I ran into financial difficulties. "Papa" Leifred, however, never let me down, and as a result, my bills never went unpaid. Until the day of his demise, I had no closer friend than Leifred Walton Johnson; may his soul rest in peace.

Until such time as the novelty of marriage wore off, Dorothy was able to set the clock by my prompt arrival from work. Then the time came for us to leave the "mountaintop and descend to the valley," in respect to life. Each morning without fail, I did my usual chores of water toting and visiting the petty shops for provisions. I also got to know the many unsavory characters on the block that readily canvassed my friendship. They, among others, would come to my residence and offer their assistance for whatever help they could render. I declined them, because if you remember, by this time I had already learned my lesson in accepting "free stuff." The woman from Gambier Village, remember her?

Whenever there was a fight or any matter pertaining to law and order, I would be called to adjudge. There were times when I was forced to leave Second Street and go to my in-laws' residence for rest and quiet.

With the passing of time and life's burdens ever increasing, I asked Mr. Noel Thompson, the staff officer, if there was any job in the Force where I could earn extra money. He said that at the Senior Officers' Mess, whenever there was a party, extra help was often required. I could offer my services there. I approached Deputy Superintendent Eric Mortemore, the wines member at the mess, who agreed to include me when the time came.

As promised, a few weeks later, I was hired to assist Constable Archie Sands, the mess steward. My initial task was to serve as a waiter. I felt most uncomfortable, as it was the first time that I had seen the majority of those gathered.

When the first couple arrived, I approached them and asked to be of assistance. Mr. Richard Ray, the director of works, required gin and tonic, while his wife ordered sherry. Constable Sands, the bartender, filled the order and I made the delivery. By this time, other guests had gathered, and as before, I obliged with drinks. After a time, I was called to the kitchen and given trays of hors d'oeuvres to serve to the guests.

When Mr. Mortemore asked me if the hors d'oeuvres had arrived, I replied, "No, sir. The horse-do-oures ain't come yet." I had no idea what he was talking about.

I was given two pounds (six dollars) for services rendered at the party's end, and I left a happy man. I made many mistakes that night and learned many a lesson. The drinks were mostly new to me, and many were thrown away because I had not remembered the exact orders. Prior to that night, I only knew of the basic hard liquors and sodas. It was certainly the first time that I had heard of the various types of mineral waters, like quinine water and club soda. I was also responsible for the breakage of many champagne glasses that night. They were made of very thin glass, and should they be deposited into a sink like cups and other hard glasses, they might all break. For that bit of advice, and for my experience that I have just shared, the Senior Officers' Mess paid dearly.

Pleased with the night's performance and happy having two extra pounds to help in balancing my budget, I mounted my bicycle and left for home. When I reached the junction of East Street and Sunlight Cottage, I observed a traffic block stretching as far away as Wulff Road. At first glance, I assumed that there was a traffic accident, and when I arrived at Milton Street, my assumption proved true. And what happened next I shall never forget.

A Human Monster

In the middle of East Street, holding two huge stones, stood a giant about six feet four inches in height and weighing approximately two hundred and thirty pounds. It was clad in short trousers, a very off coloured white T-shirt, a man's coat, and was barefoot. At its feet was a pile of stones, and at random, it was smashing cars' windshields. When my eyes beheld that sight, I thought to myself, why the hell did I not go home along Market Street? The hour of destiny had struck, for what I was lacking in size and strength I had to make up for in other areas. Then I came to the realization that there were not many areas to explore. I just had to face the onslaught of this human monster.

Depositing my cycle in a safe place, I confronted the giant, whose head was covered with a piece of discolored cloth. "Drop those stones," I shouted. (I cannot repeat the reply that came.) Then I tried to remove the stones from the hands myself, only to provoke the wrath of my opponent. It was then that I discovered that it was a woman I was dealing with. She dropped the stones, drew back her right hand, and hit me so hard in the face that I went reeling to the ground.

For the sake of my pride, I jumped to my feet—only to hit the ground again. This time, however, I cannot say whether it was her left or right hand that she decked me with. Before I was able to regain my footing, she jumped on me and woman-handled me like a toy. At training school, I was taught that the police baton was not to be used on women; however, he who offered that word of caution was a classroom teacher and not on the ground at East Street receiving kicks and blows. During the battle, bystanders were saying, "This is a good-for-nothing policeman," yet the minute I commenced using my baton, they shouted, "This is a cruel policeman, look how he is hitting the poor woman!"

The blows from my baton were landing as targeted, with negative results. The duel went on for about ten minutes before an unknown male sympathizer came to my assistance. By that time, my female attacker had taken a recess, and she calmly walked with us to a waiting car. In our efforts to get her inside the car, however, she had a change of mind. She held on to the rear door of the car and pushed it forward with such force that one of the hinges was sprained. As the sympathizer left the scene, he said, "Man, I try to help you and now I have to pay for the man taxi door."

Ezra Flowers, ex-sergeant 268, who was traveling from the Special Company Division in Oakes Field to Police Headquarters in an army truck, turned out to be the Good Samaritan who helped me with my "giant" problem. Ezra was a Bain Town boy who liked to fight, and when I was under attack from that giant human being, he appeared at the right time to lend assistance. Straightaway he sent her sprawling to her knees with a combination of blows. This time she took a mandatory eight count and did not retaliate. By that time, other police officers had arrived, and together, we lifted her into the back of the police truck and subsequently deposited her into a cell at the Southern Police Station.

At the station, we encountered Chief Inspector Edney Johnson, who told me not to be ashamed of being beaten by this woman because he had seen her beat up men much larger than me. His words brought me comfort, for after taking all that pounding, the only part of my body that was not hurting was the hairs on my head. While at the station, I learned that the giant's name was Virginia King.

I arrived home that evening around eleven thirty, after submitting my report to the corporal. Dorothy was waiting for me in the front room. "Who did you like that," she asked while inspecting me from top to bottom. I felt as though I had been pressed by a steam roller, and according to Dorothy, I looked every bit like my feelings.

The following day, Dorothy's father, Arthur "Jack" McKinney, heard about the incident and demanded to know where she had found such a worthless man who allowed a woman to beat him up. She must have defended me ably, because I was never approached and asked about it by either of my in-laws.

Monday morning at the courts, Virginia King pleaded guilty and was sent to Sandilands for seven days of observation. The doctor's report accompanying Virginia at the expiration of her remand period read, in part, that she was mentally deranged and suffered from excessive drinking. That report allowed Virginia to walk out of the court a free woman.

Determined to Advance

As I have previously stated, it was not my intention to make the Police Force my career. However, having a wife not working and expecting a child, I had to make a choice. Dorothy and I discussed it at length and decided that I should re-enlist for another three years. My education had been an informal affair, mostly gathered in the world's school of hard knocks, and as a result, I had failed the Police Proficiency Examination on two occasions. This was at a time when, if you failed one subject, you had to rewrite the examination to qualify for a promotion.

Having failed the examination for the second time, I was confronted by Deputy Commissioner Granger. He said, "I see where you failed the damn man's exams again." I quickly informed him that Constable Rigby had also failed. Mr. Granger, removing his pipe from his mouth, replied, "What the hell that supposed to mean? It only shows that you and damn Rigby are dumb alike."

Not wishing to be humiliated again by the deputy commissioner, while at the same time endeavouring to qualify myself for promotion, I sought help from those who would help me. I was told that Mr. Courtney Strachan, a most knowledgeable officer at CID, held lectures after working hours for CID constables and sub-officers. I was granted permission to attend his lectures and was successful at the next sitting of the Proficiency Examination.

Promotions were published in *Force Orders*, the weekly police publication, shortly after my exam. Success! But, I had failed to earn a place on that promotion list. I was disappointed because there were others who had superseded me.

Off-the-Wall Stories

Naturally, Dorothy asked me why I was not promoted. I was sure the truth was not forthcoming, so I substituted some off-the-wall story. Believe me, being bypassed for a promotion really hurts. Among those in the Force, it is known that a lance corporal once tried his best to get a queen-size mattress into a small suitcase after being bypassed for a promotion. After failing in his endeavor, he remarked, "What the hell happened to you today, you have been in here before." Fortunately, the lance corporal did, after a week, regain his sanity.

On another occasion, a sergeant asked me to obtain a copy of a recently published promotion list. He and another sergeant were in rivalry for a promotion to inspector. I read the list before handing it over and noted that the senior sergeant was superseded by the junior sergeant. While the two sergeants were reading the list, I witnessed the disappointed sergeant bore a hole into the back of his head with a fountain pen. In disbelief, he lost all sense of feeling and—*bam,*—blood came forth.

I know of another incident where a chief inspector refused fruits and flowers while confined to bed. He took ill after he had been overlooked for promotion. The doctor diagnosed him with a severe case of depression. Instead of fruits and flowers, he settled for toiletries (meaning toilet paper).

I thank God that over the years I learned not to take the man's promotion too seriously. If you did, you might not be able to keep your sanity when disappointments occurred, and they would occur.

Financial Challenges with Rearing our Children

On October 18, 1964, Dorothy gave birth to a baby girl. We named her Valarie Marjorie. She was a quiet baby, and at nights, my task was to make the bottles of milk. I never learned the art of changing diapers, washing, cooking, or ironing. To this day, I am unable to perform those chores, which also means that I am helpless.

We agreed that two children would suffice, a boy and a girl—but it did not quite work out that way. Allyson Vanessa was born on August 14, 1966, and Samantha Camille came four years later on March 11, 1970. We desperately wanted a Rodney Junior, but it was not to be. Today, I am grateful for my loving daughters and thank God for trusting them to our care. I don't endorse the claim, however, that "children are black people's riches." To adopt that saying as consolation for catching hell, by one who was a product of a family of eighteen, just does not add up.

To support a wife and child on a constable's salary of twelve pounds (thirty-six dollars) per month in 1964 was no joke. But everything is comparative, as forty years ago it took two people to carry ten dollars worth of groceries. Today, a five-year-old can do that. But again, we find ourselves in situations of this kind through the power of love. You get in it through love, you remain in it through love, and you triumph in it through the power of love. God is love, love is of God. You cannot see love, but it is there. It is something that is felt. You cannot see God, but he is there. Without becoming too philosophical, always remember that love is the key that opens the door to happiness. Happiness comes from within; you make yourself and those around you happy. God has given me a special gift of seeing the funny side of life and the natural ability to make others laugh. At times, I used, and still use, that gift to my advantage.

As a young lad of seven in Inagua, I would go to the white expatriates in the employ of the Salt Company, and with the assistance of my lisp tongue, I would say very fast, "Please sir/madam, lend me something, to make up something, to put with something, to buy something." Naturally, I would be asked to repeat it, and when I did, I would say it much faster, confusing the listener. Usually, because of the state of my attire, I would be given a shilling or two. By the time I was eight, I became more proficient in the art and coined a new one: "Once a fellar met a fellar in a field of beans said a fellar to a fellar, if a fellar ask a fellar, can a fellar tell a fellar what a fellar means." As you can see, I learned early in life that whatever deck the good Lord gives you; you should play it to the best of your advantage. So when faced with my financial dilemma in 1964 and beyond, I trusted in God and pressed on.

Having been married for over two years in 1966, I thought that the time had come for my family to visit my parents in Inagua. Dorothy and Val went, as planned, in mid-April, and I joined them two weeks later. My friends and family thought that my choice of a wife was sound, so they treated her with much kindness.

It was sad to bid farewell to the good people of Inagua, but Dorothy was expected to deliver our second daughter, Allyson, so we had to return to the capital. On August 14, 1966, Allyson arrived, and as before, I was in charge of the night chores, like babysitting and making bottles. But Ally was a crybaby and there were many nights when Dorothy and I would stay up, trying to pacify her.

The year 1966 saw the change in our money when we moved from pounds, shillings and pence to dollars and cents. This took some getting used to and it seemed that some things became more expensive as prices were "rounded" off to fit the new currency.

Almost two years after Allyson's birth, Dorothy secured employment at the Bahamas Telecommunications Corporation.

Our financial load became lighter, and we were able to lighten the financial strain on my mother-in-law and others. This was also around the time when I stopped eating Spam. Before I stopped, I ate it so often that I was forced to hold my breath to swallow it. This reminds me of a fellow who ate dog food every day for lunch. His doctor advised him to stop eating it because it would kill him. A few years later, the doctor noticed that the fellow was absent from his usual place at the park, so he inquired of him. He was told that the fellow had died. "I told him he would die if he kept eating dog food."

"The dog food did not kill him," was the reply. "He died from being run over by a car. He was running too fast behind a car, as usual, and the car stopped suddenly, and the car in the rear ran over him."

Of course, I could not allow Spam to cause my death. So at the first opportunity, I stopped while ahead.

Dorothy's new employment also began around the time that I became the proud owner of a 1964 red Hillman Imp. My good friend, Chief Inspector Errington Watkins, secured a loan of seven hundred pounds for me from the bank, and I made the purchase from Central Garage. I was told that the car had only one owner, an old woman living in Lyford Cay who only drove it on Saturdays to the grocery store. The Imps were small English cars made in the fashion of the Volkswagen Beatle, meaning the engine was in the rear. The difference was that the Imps had radiators for cooling water-cooled engines, while the Volkswagens were air-cooled engines. I wanted to surprise Dorothy, so I had not apprised her of my intent to make the purchase. It was on a Saturday that I took delivery of the car. It started with the first turn of the key. I drove to Second Street, Coconut Grove.

When I arrived, I invited Dorothy to get in. But she just wanted to know what fool had loaned me a car when I had no money to pay for repairs if I got into an accident. I invited her to look on the windshield to convince her that we were the owners, after which she got in. I turned the key—it wouldn't start. By that time, the garage was already closed. Dorothy began to complain that I had purchased a car that was no good. I assured her that the problem would be corrected by Monday, and then all would be well. But it was not to be. In addition to the hell Dorothy gave me over that long weekend, the car gave one problem after another. And at one point, I was scalded by boiling water from the radiator. The only thing that I did not change on that car was the body, and the only good that came from the experience was that I learned the correct name of each part of the car.

Forty-six years later, I still vividly remember the name Middleton, the Englishman I pestered every time the car, and Dorothy, gave me problems: the car won't go, and I don't know why; Dorothy won't stop raising hell, and I know why. We were spending money to service a car that we were getting little use out of, while also spending money to pay off the bank loan.

Many years ago my father told me that "the noisy wheel gets the most grease," and with that in mind, I became a nuisance to Mr. Middleton. And on one occasion, he told me so. Eventually, he offered to exchange the Imp for a used Hillman Husky, for additional money of course. I readily agreed and had Dorothy's full approval. It was then that I found out that the Imp was a self-drive; hence the problems it gave were probably the result of having too many drivers.

When the time came for my daughters Val and Ally to attend primary school, the Ministry of Education was trying to get students to attend the school nearest to their place of residence, but it never seemed to work. At one point, Val and Ally attended three different primary schools in less than two years. That was when I decided to send them to private school. Val went to Kingsway Academy and Ally to Queen's College. This created additional strain on our limited finances but we made the required sacrifice as we felt it necessary for our children's education.

We were fortunate in that our children enjoyed good heath and did not suffer from any serious illnesses that caused us any major expenses or required them to be hospitalized.

As I became more proficient in serving at the Senior Officers' Mess, the demand for my services increased. I often performed as a bartender at the senior officers' residences and filled in at the Mess when Archie Sands went on vacation or became ill. The money from these jobs went a long way to maintaining the ever-increasing bills at home.

Rodney and Dorothy at Valarie's christening, young Valarie and Allyson and youngest daughter Samantha bottom centre.

Transfer to The Senior Officers' Mess

At one point in 1964, I was asked to replace Lance Corporal Archie Sands as mess steward. Sands had received a promotion from Commissioner Morris. I declined the offer and a battle ensued.

During June 1965, Assistant Superintendent Sydney Minus, who had little regard for the English language, encouraged me to accept the job as mess steward. Mr. Minus was a kind officer, but for reasons untold, I declined his offer. He informed me that all the senior officers and party guests had requested me as Archie's replacement at the Mess.

Sometime later, Mr. George Lavell, deputy commissioner, requested that I take up the appointment. But as before, I respectfully declined. You see, I had a sound knowledge of the many duties a mess steward was required to perform. There were so many, that to compensate for the extra duties, a mess steward was given the small token of four pounds (twelve dollars) per month.

I tried as hard as possible to avoid being transferred and made a mess steward but the moment of truth was at hand, and guess what, the good-natured Mr. Noel Thompson was replaced as staff officer by none other than Mr. Watkins, alias Bumpy. I had come to know Mr. Watkins by now and felt more at ease working with him.

With Watkins, you could never be sure of his temperament; one moment he would be difficult and the next tolerant. He was, among other things, humorous and appeared to need enemies the way other men needed friends. His conduct guaranteed that he would always have plenty of both. Very few people really know Errington Watkins. Those who do, or think they do, either admire him or dislike him. They are never neutral on the subject. It's all right with Watkins if it turns out all right.

Shortly after his appointment as staff officer, Watkins summoned me to his office. "Boy," he roared, "what the hell is this! I hear you tell the people around here that you don't want to work at the Senior Officers' Mess! I know you did not say that, but instead, they misunderstood your answer because of being tied tongue." I was no longer afraid of him, having matured since my enlistment, so I stood my ground and assured him that I was not misunderstood. He shouted, "Then you should have been in the bloody cells for failing to comply with a lawful order!"

He said, "Son, let me tell you something, you catch more flies with sugar than you do with vinegar. Here it is, the people that matter in the Force, and the country, asked you to work in the Mess, and you have the nerve to refuse." Then he proceeded to give me a lecture in philosophy and afterward, I agreed to work as a mess steward.

Mr. Watkins had a reputation for getting difficult tasks to be performed throughout the Force. I suppose that after being told that I had declined a transfer to the Mess, Mr. Watkins, in his usual manner, assured the deputy commissioner that he would persuade me to go.

I was transferred from the Dispatch Office to the Senior Officers' Mess in early July 1965. Lance Corporal Archie Sands was a fairly tall man with a pencil mustache, and because of the bad texture of his hair, he kept his head almost in a state of baldness. He remained at the Mess for two days after my transfer. I received a warm welcome from both the regular and honourary members at my new assignment. The regulars were Commissioner of Police Mr. Nigel Godfrey Morris; Deputy Commissioner Mr. George Lavell,; Assistant Commissioners Albert Joel Miller and Stanley Ridell Moir; Superintendents E. James Bryan, Leslie Roberts, and John Thomas Crawley; Deputy Superintendents Eric Mortemore, Leslie Cates, Robert Oldham, Dennis Morgan, Gerald Augustus Bartlett, Salathiel

Harvey Thompson, Greg Bentley, Frank Sager, and Wilson B. Wilson; Assistant Superintendents Sydney Minus, Sigfred Wilson, Courtney Strachan, Noel Thompson, and Edney Hanlon Johnson.

The honourary members were Mr. Gerald Christopher Cash; Mr. Richard Ray, director of the Ministry of Works; Father William Granger, prison chaplain; Superintendent Byron Pinder; Drs. John Lunn, Cecil Bethell, Stanley Cooper, Gordon Leam, Cleveland Eneas and Earl Farrington; Mr. Oscar Phillips; Honourable Roy M. Solomon; and others whose names I cannot recall.

Deputy Superintendent Eric Mortemore was the wines member; as such, he was responsible for the Mess' operation. He was also the Force's communications officer and hailed from Crayford Kent, England. He enlisted in the Force on September 19, 1959, with the rank of deputy superintendent, after serving in the Malaya Police Service. Mr. Mortemore was a good organizer and bubbled with positive ideas. He did not encourage small talk and would go to extraordinary lengths to save the Mess a few pence. Mr. Mortemore also made certain that I knew that he was in charge. In very short order, I came to learn the members' dispositions and, as Mr. Watkins encouraged, I went the extra mile to please.

The day before I assumed my new duties at the Mess, Mr. Watkins told me that he could promise me nothing in respect to a promotion; however, he said that if I performed satisfactorily, he would sing my praises.

A Promotion

With the voice of angels and the instrument of gold, my praises must have been heralded, for on August 1, 1965, I was summoned to Mr. Watkins' office where he presented me with an envelope. The letter enclosed stated that the commissioner was pleased to approve my promotion to lance corporal and that he wished me all the best for the future. I thanked Mr. Watkins most sincerely for the high degree of confidence he and the commissioner placed in me and promised to do my best in serving him and the Force.

After leaving his office, I visited Stores and had my stripe mounted on my tunic. From that moment, I walked around with my shoulder hoisted as though I suffered from a boil under my arm. On learning of my good fortune, members of the Mess congratulated me and assured me of their support. Dorothy was overjoyed with my promotion; however, her joy turned to disappointment when I told her that the promotion only came with seven extra shillings per week.

My promotion brings to mind the two prayers that a Baptist minister can say when he is called on during festive occasions to give thanks for the food that is offered:

(1) if the plate in which the meal sits is not running over, he prays, "Lord, we thank you for that which we are about to receive"; and

(2) when the plate overflows with food, he says, "Most Heavenly Father, we, your humble children, give you thanks for that which you so graciously provided from your bountiful store."

I dare not guess which one of these prayers Dorothy offered. But as the lord bishop, the retired Right Reverend Michael Eldon, would say, "Thank God for small mercies."

Mr. Watkins' stay as staff officer came to an end the day after my promotion was announced in *Force Orders* on August 2, 1965. He was sent to the Traffic Division as second in command. Inspector Reginald Deane Dumont took his place as staff officer.

Duties of a Mess Steward

I quickly settled in at the Mess and enjoyed my new job immensely. The officers and honourary members took advantage of the available facilities including lawn tennis, table tennis, darts, card games and the showing of movies which was a regular feature on Wednesday nights. I was made to feel a part of it. It was believed that Mr. Gerald Cash and Mr. Oscar Phillips, the honourary consul for Guyana, were the senior members of the group, followed by Drs. John Lunn, Cecil Bethell, and Earl Farrington.

The duties of a mess steward were as follows: Monday through Saturday, report for duty at eight a.m. and prepare to serve beverages to gazetted officers and their guests; then, after washing cups and glasses, deliver cases of beers, liquor, sodas and cigarettes to the homes of the officers who were residing in the barracks. These deliveries were made on foot with the steward carrying the beverage cases on his shoulders. At one p.m., or whenever, the steward reported off duty and returned again at four thirty to serve beverages and hors d'oeuvres. Most nights, the steward would perform until eleven thirty and, at times, after midnight. Wednesday nights, movies were shown and the officers' wives and guests would attend. Periodically, dinner and cocktail parties were held. There were times when a steward would remain at the Mess from eight a.m. until midnight. For every party or dinner, the steward had the Herculean task of cleaning the many pieces of silver given to the Mess. The Mess account preparation and the ordering of supplies also came under the portfolio of the steward

At the close of 1965, the tennis group had a party at the Mess, and I was presented with a gift of over thirty pounds for services rendered. Additionally, I received five pounds from Mr. Gerald Cash. Mr. Cash, throughout my sojourn as a mess steward, demonstrated kindness and compassion, and he often gave me gifts of money after the Saturday evening parties. I had the highest regard for him, as both a legislator and as a person. He had been connected with the Force in one capacity or another for over thirty years, and he was respected by all he came into contact with. Although this good gentleman, in later years, reached the highest position in the Commonwealth of The Bahamas, that of governor general, and received a knighthood from Her Majesty, the Queen, he could still be found on Saturday evenings sitting around the tennis court at Police Headquarters in camaraderie with the tennis group. From woman born, there could hardly be a greater statesman than he.

One Wednesday night in January, 1966, during the viewing of a movie in the Mess, Mr. Leslie Roberts, the training school commandant, ordered drinks for all those present and said that I could have one as well. I always fancied a drink known in the Mess as "Cash's Special," and I thought that this was the golden opportunity to have one legally. The concoction included V.S.O.P. Brandy, Tia Maria, and milk, served with crushed ice. The drink was served in a tall water goblet, and to create the proper effect, the drink must be doubled.

When I returned with my drink, and before starting the projector, Mr. Roberts asked, "Burrows, what the hell is that you drinking?"

"Cash's Special," I said.

"What!" he shouted. "That damn thing costs five bobs [shillings]. I did not mean for you to get something that expensive. That damn drink cost more than my own." The patrons laughed, and I am sad to say that that was the first and last time that I received a drink from the commandant.

Mr. Dennis Morgan, the band's colourful director, was another fan of mine. This officer came to The Bahamas on September 3, 1959, after a distinguished career in the Regimental Band of the Worcestershire Regiment in the British Army. Having registered in the service while still a boy, he was trained to play the clarinet. He fought with courage and distinction during the war and earned a Military Medal (also known as an MM). Mr. Morgan was a friend to all, and if he had a fault, it was his generosity in purchasing drinks for others. He would come to the Mess at opening hours and would often leave long after the others. We would play darts or converse long into the night.

The sixties were years of fun, and the Mess was a place of infectious laughter. The merriment increased when Mr. Watkins was promoted to Assistant Superintendent on July 1,1966 which permitted him to become a member of the senior officers' mess.

He would often chide other officers about their dress. He once informed a newly made officer, who attended a Mess function clad in silver trousers and a plaid jacket, that he was now a senior officer and should therefore not be seen in clothing fit for those who hunted seals. He said, "John, you are too damn pretty tonight. You must be going seal hunting."

Later that night, the offended officer said, "Burrows, you know Watkins should not make a joke like that in front of all those people." I comforted him by telling him that those present understood Watkins' ways, and as a result, he should not be offended. You see, I was now in Watkins' corner. After all, he had seen to it that I received a stripe.

Wherever there was action of any sort, Mr. Watkins would be present, and April 27, 1965, was no exception, the day known in Bahamian history as "Black Tuesday." A huge crowd had gathered near the House of Parliament, where an important piece of legislation was being debated. It was the largest group of demonstrators I had ever seen. On such occasions, all available police officers are sent to assist with crowd control, and that is how I found myself among the ranks with members of the Pay Office staff.

Lance Corporal Fynes and I happened to report together to Mr. Watkins at the scene, and the first thing he did was to relieve us of the canes we were carrying. He said that if we did not know how to use canes, then we should not be carrying them. Naturally, in accordance with his reputation, he used a number of adjectives to describe how sloppy and dumb we looked, obviously because of the large gathering. The scene was swarming with people, such that Magistrate John Bailey, an Irishman, attempted to read the riot act from the top of a patrol car.

That day was the first time that I had seen Watkins in action, and I admired his courage, energy, and forcefulness. There were times when he bent the Force's rules out of shape to achieve his objectives, but the end results were always "mission accomplished."

I also made the effort to get to know Mr. Salathiel Thompson, a reserved officer who listened more and spoke less, for good measure. The latter was not a frequent visitor to the Mess, for he was a teetotaller, but I knew that he was destined for greatness from the favourable comments I had gleaned from those who controlled the destiny of men.

As a trusted bartender, I often heard a lot of things. But as a sensible bartender, I did not speak that which I heard. As my father once said, "Son, the good Lord in his infinite wisdom gave unto men two ears and only one mouth for a purpose, which is because he wants you to hear more and talk less."

During June 1966 my brother Ural came to visit us from Inagua. At the end of his holiday, he decided not to return home. Instead, he solicited my assistance in securing a job. I immediately petitioned Mr. Oscar Phillips, who straightaway obliged by offering Ural a post at Crown Lands as a chainman. My brother, however, only worked there for just over two months. He informed me that a "chainman" was a glorified name for a person who was handy with a machete (cutlass). His job was to clear bush to allow the surveyors to operate. With some persuasion, I convinced him to enlist as a direct entry into the fire services—because of his height. He was shorter than me by half of an inch.

Mr. John Thomas Crawley succeeded Mr. Eric Mortemore as wines member during the winter of 1966, and like the latter, Mr. Crawley was a pleasure to work with. He gave me much latitude to operate, and for him, I tried my best.

As time went by, I became weary with working at the Mess, so I requested a transfer. Nearly all the officers asked me to stay, but I wanted to get on with my career. Many told me that I was making a big mistake by asking to go when the members wanted me to remain. Mr. Morgan petitioned the authorities to promote me to sergeant and to have me remain in the post. I am happy, however, that the recommendation did not come to fruition.

The Reign of the Three Ms

My personal life took a dramatic turn in 1966 and I was convinced that marriage and a career were compatible. It was a time when the three Ms - Morris, Miller and Moir-reigned supreme in the Force and therefore it was advantageous that they knew you. Commissioner Morris was in charge of the Force. Mr. Miller was assistant commissioner in charge of the uniform branch and Mr. Moir was assistant commissioner, criminal investigation department.

I was very fortunate to know the three Ms and they in turn knew me. This however is not to suggest that I was given preferential consideration when the time came for promotion but they all could have vouched for my ability, integrity and devotion to duty at all times. Working at the senior officer's mess had its advantages as it afforded me the opportunity to be observed by the three Ms. By now, I had also come to realize that if you were deficient in one area, it was important for you to make it up in another. Therefore I got to know these three gentlemen and I went the extra mile to please them.

The Royal Visit

The year 1966 started with a royal visit. The Bahamas was graced with the visit of Her Majesty, Queen Elizabeth II, in January 1966. I am proud to say that I was a member of the honour guard that Her Majesty inspected after disembarking from the royal yacht *Britannia*, berthed at Prince George Dock. I will never forget that auspicious occasion.

Mr. Gerald Bartlett was the parade commandant, Mr. Keith Mason was right marker, and Mr. McFerris Hanna, who was also a member of the guard, reported for duty late. Before the formation of the guard, Hanna was seen running across Bay Street at full throttle with his helmet spike and chain in his hand. That Hanna's dimension may be computed in cubics is an indication of his bulk. Having galloped to the area where the guard was to be drawn up, Hanna remarked, "Boys, these damn laundries should all burn down. I put this tunic in there from last week and I just got it out a little while ago." After mopping his huge face (the perspiration automatically disappeared from his bald head), he proceeded to put on his helmet.

He was surprised when Lance Corporal Akel Clarke asked him what had happened to his helmet's badge. Striking his helmet where his badge was usually attached, Hanna said, "Oh, lord. What happened to my badge? Clarke, you think Mrs. Majesty will see that?"

Clarke replied, "Chief, you are a big man, so therefore, the Queen may ask you what happened to your badge."

"Well give me your badge!" Hanna said.

At the conclusion of the parade, one of the officers asked Hanna what Her Majesty had said about his missing badge. Hanna laughed and said, "In this Force, you must be smart.

When the woman was nearing me, I held my head high and focused my eyes toward the sky. While passing me, she must have said, 'That officer must be half crazy, looking toward the sky as though he heard a message.' I did not hear a message. What I did in fact see was orderly room staring me straight in the face." With that, the area became a place of infectious laughter.

Transfer Back to the Records Department

Finally, on November 19, 1966, Dorothy's birthday, I was transferred from the Mess back to the Records Department. Before my departure, the Tennis Group held a small Saturday afternoon party in my honour and presented me with a gift of fifteen pounds.

I shall never forget such an occasion. When it came time for the master of ceremonies to speak, he began by saying, "Gentlemen, you may not believe it, but Strachan will be a big miss over here."

Mr. Albert Miller, on hearing this, said, "Who the hell is this party in honour of?"

The master of ceremonies then said, "You all just wait and see; we will never get another Mess man like Hepburn." After much talk and laughter, the master of ceremonies was told by Mr. Cash that my name was Burrows. He agreed and finally said, "You all know what I mean. I mean there will never be another steward in this Mess like Lightbourn." Well that was the end of the party, and to the sound of fun and laughter, I handed over the duties of mess steward to Constable Benjamin Ferguson, a native of San Salvador. Constable Ferguson, who exited the Force at the expiration of his contract on March 16, 1970, is now a member of the cloth. Dr. Ferguson was always a studious person, so it is not surprising that he has gained great altitude in his call to the sacred ministry.

On my return to Headquarters and reassignment to the Records Department, I met acting Chief Inspector Lawrence Major, the new staff officer. Mr. Major had assumed this position from Chief Inspector Reginald Deane Dumont on August 1, 1966.

Mr. Major, a Moss Town, Exuma, native, joined the Force on August 29, 1950, where he rose steadily through the ranks. He was later selected to head the Marine Division of the Force at a time when it was suffering growing pains, and his contribution to the formation of this new section was invaluable. For his loyal and dedicated service, Mr. Major received due recognition from Her Majesty the Queen with the award of the Queen's Police Medal (QPM). While working with him, I had found Mr. Major to be a gentleman. He had a razor-sharp mind and a determination to succeed as a staff officer. He was a man whose contributions to the Force have been acknowledged and he retired with a senior rank.

One Saturday evening while working together, Mr. Major and I left the Coral Harbour canal on a fishing trip in a ten- or twelve-foot boat. Shortly after reaching the fishing grounds, the winds shifted to the northwest and the sea got rough. Being the knowledgeable seaman that he was, Mr. Major requested that I pull the anchor into the craft. He started the borrowed Seagull engine, and then we were on our way.

Shortly thereafter, the engine began to sputter and it eventually failed completely. Mr. Major's efforts to restart the engine proved fruitless, and as a result, my boss got out the oars and started to row (burn pine). With both wind and heavy seas against us, and despite Mr. Major's gallant efforts, he made little progress. After half an hour's labour, Mr. Major asked me for relief, only to have me tell him that the only thing I was unable to do in a boat was scull. He said, "Why was I not told that before we left the land?"

"Because you did not ask," I answered.

Mr. Major was a man of long patience, so he did not show his anger at my answer. Our misfortune occurred around seven p.m., and it was not until eleven that I arrived home. A week later, jokingly, I suggested to Mr. Major that we venture on another fishing trip. With his usual broad smile he replied, "When you learn to scull, we may go every Saturday." That was our first and final trip off New Providence together.

The year 1967, throughout The Bahamas, was one of jubilation and thanksgiving for the masses. For on January 10,

1967, the Progressive Liberal Party wrested the government from the United Bahamian Party. That is all I will say on the subject, for an African friend I met in Hendon, England, in September 1972 told me that there were two topics that should always be left to the experts—politics and religion—because at the end of a debate on both subjects, no one wins.

My friend Mr. Major, on September 18, 1967, having been promoted to the rank of acting assistant superintendent, was transferred to head the Central Division. He was replaced by a chief inspector I had little respect for. Shortly after this man's appointment, I realized that he possessed an enormous appetite for gossip. I had not met any man who depressed me as much as this officer. He was the one man that I most actively disliked, and the feeling was reciprocated in full measure. I knew that I would have trouble the moment he was appointed. For all intents and purposes, he lived the life of a Nassau playboy, travelling frequently and pursuing a succession of girls attracted to his easy money. The only thing he seemed to cherish more than gin and tonic was more gin and tonic, and because of his love for women, liquor, and money, which have proven to be man's destruction for centuries, he found himself, most days, fighting a losing battle with sleep.

Throughout the world, it is an established fact that rank has its privileges. The Police Force was no exception. I was often asked to make purchases for those in authority while I was out on dispatch duties. Each day, the commissioner's private secretary would ask me to collect her lunch from the Carlton House Hotel, situated on East Street, and I would always agree. Before I did, I always sought and was granted permission from the staff officer, who, when I asked, said that he saw no reason for me to ask to perform such a favour. However, three weeks later, I was more than surprised when the commissioner's chauffeur told me that I should stop running errands for Headquarters staff. He then explained that the staff officer had said that all I did all day was run errands for people. While he was telling me this, the staff officer walked into the office—and the chauffeur kept talking, set on delivering his message. To this day, I have the greatest respect for that chauffeur.

Because it was nearing lunchtime, I waited until two before I approached the staff officer and the commissioner's secretary about the lunch arrangement. Naturally, the staff officer denied making the remarks he did. As faith, luck, or prayers would have it (I know not which), this staff officer's stay at Headquarters was short-lived anyway, for on September 11, 1967, he was posted to the Traffic Division. I also remember other unpleasant experiences I had with this man, but in the interest of time and space, I hereby close the chapter on the life and memory of this deceased officer . May he rest in peace and be judged accordingly.

Chilean Eleazor Turner, a veteran police officer, became the new staff officer. He and I became friends from the start, and thereafter, we worked in harmony. Turner was a man who spoke his mind on any subject, whether it hurt friend or foe. He once told me that it was one thing to suspect the truth, but that it was another to hear it from a man's lips. He was noted for his far-fetched stories, the love he had for horse racing, and his famous saying: "Boy, don't cause me to swear."

Turner's devotion to his family was unquestionable, and he saw to it that his children received the best education that he was able to afford. He never ate lunch; instead, he played darts with Chief Inspector Vernon Wilkinson and others during the lunch hour. He was a fine officer and a gentleman, whose contributions to the Force have not in my opinion been adequately acknowledged.

1968 General Election

Prior to Mr. Turner's last posting, I had the pleasure of working with him throughout the Crooked Island District during the April, 1968 general election. During my tour of duty in the Crooked Island constituency, I was given the opportunity to witness the fine art of Out Island policing under the tutelage of Chief Inspector Turner. On the day of the election, Mr. Turner and I were stationed in Acklins; I was at Pompey Bay where I had many relatives, and Mr. Turner moved around throughout the constituency.

At the Pompey Bay All-Age School where I was posted, Mr. H. O. Ferguson, an election agent and also a native of Acklins, withdrew a ruler from his pocket and proceeded to take measurements of the ballot box just before the voting began. He even measured the inside of the box. On completion of this strange act, Turner asked Ferguson to explain the rationale behind the measurement taking. He said, "Son, you won't understand. That is a bit deep fer yinna [for you] to fathom." In Turner's opinion, only Ferguson and God could fathom what had taken place.

Once voting got started, complaints of all types were reported. One was this: a woman produced receipts from the mate of a local mail boat that stated that Asa H. Pritchard had sent groceries to her aboard the boat. The woman's groceries could not be found. Therefore, she petitioned the captain, who was a native of Acklins and whose reputation and name were synonymous with the mysterious disappearances of other people's things on board his vessel.

To satisfy the old soul, I left on inquiry with her. I saw and questioned the captain in her presence. He said, "Officer, you suppose to be a sensible man. You ever hear of a boat that ate grocery?" The old woman wept bitterly.

What fascinated me most about Acklins was the roof of the schoolhouse. I felt that it was the steepest roof ever to be found in the world. I have journeyed to many places, and I have yet to see the likes of it. Sir Christopher Wren, the great architect of English fame, I am sure, would marvel at such an incredible piece of architecture. The roof was so steep that a bird would encounter difficulties standing on it.

My stay in Acklins was pleasant, and my relatives treated me well. When the ballots were counted and the sun had long since disappeared from view, the returning officer Mr. Curtis Tynes, Mr. Turner, Mr. H. O. Ferguson, and I departed Pompey Bay for the journey to Crooked Island. HO, as Ferguson was called, left the vehicle when we arrived at Delectable Bay, his place of abode. On leaving the truck, Ferguson appeared to have been swallowed up by the bushes, for there was no road that led him home.

We arrived at the Cove, Mr. Turner, Mr. Tynes and I, with the ballot boxes at about ten p.m., after being ferried from the settlement of Lovely Bay. While waiting for the vehicle to transport us to Colonel Hill, we learned the election results from the radio. Mr. Turner said that I was a straight dreamer, for on the night before the elections, I dreamed that the Progressive Liberal Party (PLP) won the government. Mr. Turner, whose first love was to fatten the bank accounts of those who operated the Hobby Horse Hall Racetrack, asked me to inform him of all the dreams and nightmares that I might have. For, according to him, I must have been Joseph of biblical times and he, Pharoah. I told Turner that Joseph received great rewards for his services; therefore, I wanted to know what I would receive for my own. It was only a joke, but I would do all within my power to oblige my friend Chilean Turner.

As we continued to wait for transportation, we passed the time by killing sand flies, mosquitoes, and horseflies. The vehicle finally arrived around eleven fifteen p.m. We arrived at Colonel Hill hungry, thirsty, and weary, so we inquired about food. Local Constable John Delevaux, with whom we were residing, said that it was much too late for him to prepare food;

he could only offer biscuits and tea. Some thirty minutes later, between sleep and wake, we consumed the tea and biscuits that had been so slowly prepared. For the remainder of that night of slumber, my roaming spirit took me back to my place of birth, where I relived my childhood days.

I woke on the morning of the eleventh with renewed vigor and strength to the melodious sounds of birds and the light and gentle breeze rustling the leaves of the trees at the top of Colonel Hill. As I sat quietly on a wall enjoying that which God had so graciously created, my thoughts drifted back to the week before when the old DC-3 plane had landed on Crooked Island and the officer with the ballot boxes had disembarked: how on the journey to Colonel Hill, the truck that I rode in was not allowed to proceed because the driver in an approaching truck refused to pull to the side of the narrow, white road; how the young constables who made up the detail had dressed themselves in their finest garments, only to be told that the only form of recreation was the killing of insects; and how, a few days later, a young police constable, who had never visited an Out Island, became homesick and wept to his heart's content.

I also remembered how the proprietor, Constable John Delevaux, had turned the generator off at ten p.m., and when we complained that the heat was unbearable with the fans turned off, he replied, "Which one do you like, the heat or mosquitoes? Open the house and get bit, or keep it closed and endure the heat." The consensus was that we endured the heat. I thought about the night of the ninth at Acklins, how an approaching vehicle's lights shone into the bushes, rather than onto the road.

On further inspection of the vehicle, Mr. Turner asked to visit the factory that manufactured that type of contraption. The vehicle, as it turned out, had been involved in a serious accident that left the chassis bent.

Then there was Louise "Ma" Chisholm, the proprietor of a small general store on Crooked Island. It was at this store that I got the impression that a lead pencil sharpened automatically if one put it in his or her mouth. For each time this dear, old woman wrote two words, she would then put the joint of the pencil into her mouth. It seemed like the price list for her stock must have been posted in the sky, for each time she was asked the price of an article, she would look up to the heavens and answer,

"No pound, no shilling, six pence." The currency had been changed for almost two years but Ma was reliving the past.

At about eight fifteen in the morning, Lance Corporal Thomas "Chief" Greenslade, one of the most efficient switchboard operators the Force has ever had, and the father of the present Commissioner Ellison Greenslade, came and sat beside me. "Chief," as Greenslade was called, kept close companion with an ever-burning King Edward cigar. He must have earned his alias from his habit of addressing everyone as "Chief," and I was no exception. He shouted, "Beautiful morning, hey Chief!" I bowed my head in agreement. With my trend of thought thus broken, Chief and I joked about the week's activities until we were summoned to breakfast.

The ballot recount was conducted at the schoolhouse in Colonel Hill, and then the ten officers including Mr. Turner and I were driven to the airport to await the arrival of the aircraft. While there, we were entertained by an ex-police officer named Kendal Farquharson, alias Bush Crack.

Farquharson played an accordion while a native girl flirted with the surrounding policemen, a category I did not fall into. I have yet to meet another group of people who have as little as the people of Crooked Island and who enjoy life as much as they do. As we boarded the airplane with the ballot boxes and our personal effects, I could not help but marvel over the many thousands of people who would travel to the cities in search of happiness, only to discover later that they had left happiness behind when they left Crooked Island.

Around eleven a.m., we departed Crooked Island. From the plane's windows, we could still see those gathered to bid us bon voyage waving and clapping. We landed in the capital two hours later than expected. I helped escort the ballot boxes to the Parliamentary Registrar's office, and then I left for home.

My family was very happy to receive me; absence really did make the heart grow fonder. I was allowed two days off duty for the period that I spent at Crooked Island.

Upgrade to Records Clerk

Upon my return to work following my tour of duty in the Crooked Island District, I was upgraded from dispatch officer to records clerk. Upon my upgrading to records clerk, Constable Thomas Hamilton, alias Panic, performed the dispatch duties. He later sustained serious injuries from a motorcycle accident and was replaced by Constable Howard Lightbourn, alias Magoo.

The staff officer, Turner, who was never destined to be a diplomat or a politician, and Lightbourn, who was quiet and shy, supplied the office with fun and laughter. Both Turner and Lightbourn loved to play the horses and both, from all appearanccs, enjoyed their losses. After each track meet, they would compare their losing tickets and remark how they could have caught the daily double if they had only followed a certain dream or had bought their dead grandmothers' ages. Each morning that I reported for duty, Turner would ask me whether I dreamed the night before. He would be disappointed when I said no, and he would often ask me if I only dreamed when it was a general election.

Besides loving the horses, Turner loved jokes. Each day he would tell a different one, even though it might be at his own expense. One time he joked about the time that he ran into a casuarina tree on Bay Street where a number of mirrors were posted. On approaching one of the mirrors, he saw his car's reflection but mistook it for another car coming directly at him. He tried his best to avoid hitting the oncoming vehicle (his own) and ended up running into the tree. After the accident, Turner said that he looked for the car he swerved to avoid, but he could not find it.

Change in Command

On June 13, 1968, the Force heralded the appointment of Mr. Thomas Edwin Clunie as its eighth commissioner. Mr. Clunie, who was English by birth, came to the Force from the Royal Hong Kong Police Force, where he had served as an assistant commissioner. His inaugural address to the Force appeared in *Force Orders* no. 27, on June 24, 1968. If by chance you should get the opportunity, you should read and digest it. I can write volumes in respect to Mr. Clunie's term in office, but *Destiny* must be more about me and less about him. Therefore, suffice it to say that, to me, he was charitable and did much to help me on the way to greater things.

Mr. Turner's tenure as staff officer came to an end on July 4, 1968, when he left the colony to attend a senior officer's course at Bramshill Police College in England.

The job of staff officer, which I in due course so ably mastered, was learned at the feet of Chief Inspector Turner's successor, Mr. Alonzo Maxwell Butler. Butler, who also enjoyed a chief inspector's status, was good to be around but hard to work for. After assuming his new assignment and giving his maiden speech, I told him that my best would be forthcoming. He replied, "Not your best. What I want is your first best." I thought to myself, what manner of man is this?

As a staff officer, Mr. Butler was a good choice. He was a sensible, level-headed officer who was thorough in his reasoning, fluent in speech, and exemplary with the pen. Loyalty, versatility, and reliability were his greatest attributes; he was a strict law-and-order man, a policeman who could, and would, always produce results.

In the Police Force, you are told that if you wish to move upward, then you must report for duty clean, on time, and you must comply with all lawful orders. There was also other criteria, and I endeavoured to ascertain what it was. What I found was that you must have at least one person in the hierarchy who knows you well and who would vouch for your suitability for an upgrade.

First Force Education Officer

The first force education officer Mr. Burket Kniveton, was appointed on June 1, 1965. He came to the Force from the Ministry of Education and was exceptionally well-qualified. It was thought that such an appointment would enormously benefit the Force. Mr. Kniveton, however, was too high-powered and educated for the regular rank and file, whose requirements were basic education in English language, report writing, simple mathematics, and general knowledge subjects.

The saintly-looking gentleman, a former priest, who was referred to as the "bearded one," was a short, thin-looking man whose appearance called to mind one of Jesus' disciples. When he entered the Force, I had the opportunity to serve him at the Senior Officers' Mess. His entry also coincided with the arrival of a new brand of liquor called "Old Oak." Like a true Anglican who did not hide to take his booze, Mr. Kniveton would enter the Mess at five p.m. and order Old Oak and water. How a man can drink rum chased with water is beyond me. But my unassuming friend seemed to encounter no problem when consuming his favourite brew. In fact, it was hilarious to watch Mr. Kniveton hold the glass to his head for such a long time on the last gulp. No other priest could have consumed the end residue of a sacramental wine from mass with greater religious fervor than Mr. Kniveton.

I can remember the first class Mr. Kniveton held very well. It was an introductory class to determine the level of competence of those who volunteered to attend. The room in

Arthur's House was so packed with policemen that there was only standing room. Those gathered were raring to go , but I am sad to say that with the passing of days, the numbers attending classes dwindled. As my father would say, "Only the strong survive." I did not last very long. I was gone on the second day. The next day, Mr. Kniveton approached me to determine why I was no longer attending classes. I advised him that the demands of the job did not permit me to continue, which was the truth, but not the whole truth. The truth of the matter was my inability to master the difficult subject of mathematics, which was a required course.

One person I shall always remember from that class was Assistant Superintendent James W. Allen. Allen was a dedicated public servant who was not too bright, but nevertheless, he came. He was, by far, the oldest member of the class, and like me, he came with the idea of earning a few more dollars. (This was at a time when an education allowance was being paid to those who possessed certificates of worth. Unfortunately for us, we did not qualify, as Allen did not possess a first-aid certificate and I did not possess a health certificate.)

On clear nights, Mr. Kniveton, who resided in the police compound, could be found studying the stars with the aid of a sextant. Assistant Superintendent Allen, who was about to make his departure from the classroom because of his inability to cope, said to me one day, "Burrows, we must be bad off. That damn man Mr. Kniveton can read the stars in heaven, and we can't read the map of Nassau." Before we parted company that day, Allen told me that he could no longer put up with Mr. Kniveton's foolishness, and that was the end of Allen the student.

As I previously mentioned, Mr. Kniveton was too high-powered academically for the majority of his student's shallow wits, and as a result, it cannot be said that he filled the role for which he was hired. He retired on December 29, 1967. On July 12, 1968, Mr. Errol E. D. Lawrence became the second Force education officer.

Hospital Admission

On July 1, 1968, in true style and much fanfare, Commissioner Clunie announced his first promotion, and guess what; I was upgraded to a full corporal. Dorothy was elated and I was exceedingly glad. I also had two other reasons for jubilation: Dorothy, on May 28, 1968, received employment with the Bahamas Telecommunications Corporation; and in June, my good friend Mr. Watkins stood as guarantor for me at a bank for the loan of one thousand dollars to purchase a motor car.

Then tragedy struck. I became ill and as a result, I visited the police surgeon, Dr. Roland Cumberbatch. This good doctor was advanced in years and habitually carried a brown leather bag. He was a short man who was not overly endowed with the virtue of patience. Whatever your complaint, he would prescribe a tablet called APC. I never determined what the letters stood for, but in police circles it meant "All Police Cure."

On entering the office, Dr. Cumberbatch, who looked like he smelled an unpleasant odor, growled, "What you say wrong with you now?" I informed him that my rear end was constantly paining me, and as a result, I could not sit. He then proceeded to examine me. Afterward, he wrote on a piece of paper and tore it from a legal pad. While passing it to me, he said, "Go and see Dr. Farrington at his clinic in three weeks time."

"But Doc," I said, "I can't sit down."

And Cumberbatch hastily replied, "If you had eaten the correct food, you would be able to sit down." Then I asked him the nature of my illness, and he told me that that was the reason why I had to go see Dr. Farrington. As a boy of five years, I was taught a poem that ably describes Dr. Cumberbatch, but it is best that I not repeat it here.

Leaving Dr. Cumberbatch's office in pain and confusion, and bearing the piece of paper addressed to Dr. Earl Farrington in my hand, I stopped at the bottom of the steps leading into Arthur's House to ponder my next move. Realizing that the pain would become unbearable over the next two weeks, and remembering the offer Dr. Farrington made while I was his bartender at the Senior Officers' Mess, I immediately left for Princess Margaret Hospital. On my arrival, the secretary informed me that Dr. Farrington would not see me without an appointment. I told her that he would if she announced my presence. Reluctantly, she informed the good doctor, and he acceded to my request.

A painful man is a persistent man, and a persistent man gets results. A short time later, Dr. Farrington appeared at the door and invited me into his office.

Dr. Farrington examined me and diagnosed my complaint as fistula. I would need surgery to have it corrected. After Dr. Farrington went to great lengths to explain the origin of my complaint, I hastily agreed to undergo the operation. Having informed Dorothy, my pessimist, of what the doctor had said, she said quietly, "What all will they be cutting out?" She agreed to the operation after I assured her that the fistula was not in that arca.

On August 6, 1968, at nine a.m., I was admitted to the Princess Margaret Hospital where I was prepped for surgery. Like a man who must keep his appointment with destiny, all that day I listened to my mortal brothers who had already been operated on and those who were awaiting similar fates. Some were praying for me, while others told me how painful I would feel once the morphine effect had died down.

One man I shall never forget was the chap whose bottom lip weighed far in excess of four pounds. His fame had spread both far and wide as a "breeder." But he did not breed animals. He concentrated heavily on breeding children. On his demise, he was eulogized as fathering more than fifty children. While lying on his bed of affliction, a little boy appeared during visiting hours and yelled, "Daddy." Even though the boy was only about eight years of age, there was no question who his father was, for his bottom lip, even at that tender age, would have weighed almost that of his father's. The lad went on to say, "Mama say if you gat anything to send this week?"

"Well gad damn," my big-lip friend said. "Even in hospital they will haunt you! Boy, what ya ma name?"

"Emma," he replied.

"Emma from where?"

"From the Grove," the boy answered quickly.

Staring at the ceiling for a few seconds, my friend then retrieved twenty dollars from under his pillow and said, "Emma, that is possible. Here son, take this to ya ma." After the boy's departure, we all enjoyed a good laugh over seeing a man who identified his son by asking him who his mother was.

This man is now deceased. However, those of you who are old enough may know of whom I write. I was once told that he and another man had a row, and for a time, my hospital friend seemed to have the upper hand. But then the other remarked, "G——, who does wear your clean clothes?" I often pondered the same question.

As usual, I have strayed. Forgive me!

On the morning of August 7, like a condemned man who was to keep his appointment with Father Time, I awaited mine with Dr. Farrington. According to the hospital gossip, Dr. Clinton Thomas was the best bone surgeon, but Dr. Farrington was the overall best—whatever that meant. It did not really matter; I had explicit faith in Farrington. I was prepared for an eventuality. Or so I thought.

At about ten a.m., a short, bright attendant entered the ward pushing a trolley. The word "GENERAL" was written in bold letters on his white uniform. Stopping near my bed, he said, "Burrows, are you ready?"

I answered, "Yes, but first let me pee."

Prior to seeing General, I was ready. But after seeing him, I started to change my mind. You see, he was clad in all white, wearing a pair of water boots, and his head and mouth were covered. If my memory serves me right, he also had a few medals attached to his jacket. He truly resembled a general, even though he appeared to have been serving with the Salvation Army.

Eventually my fears subsided, and I was wheeled into the operating room and placed behind a curtain. A Dr. Graham gave me an injection and thereafter I felt like a general myself, like I was at the top of the world. The wait for Dr. Farrington felt like eternity. Then General suddenly appeared. This time, however, he appeared ready for an attack.

After General assured me that I was in capable hands and had nothing to fear, he rolled me into the operating theatre. Once inside, Dr. Graham led me into a lively conversation to distract me while he tied a piece of plastic around my arm. He then gave me another injection, and as he slowly removed the hose, I faded slowly away into the great unknown. Very late that afternoon, and with the aid of a nurse's slaps, I awoke and asked if it was over. The nurse told me it was and I fell back asleep relieved. The following morning, I suffered severe pain and almost fainted when the nurse placed me into a tub of salt and water. That daily ritual was to speed up the healing process. It proved successful, for in seven days I was allowed to return home.

During my sojourn in hospital, Dr. Farrington visited me each day. Before he left one day, I asked him for my bill, since I had visited his clinic prior to the operation as a private patient. He said, "Mr. Burrows, it was a pleasure to be of assistance to you. It is not over yet, because you are required to attend my clinic until the healing process is satisfactory." Today, I see Dr. Farrington as the kind man who enriches life. His cause is people. So sincere. So vital. When was there a kinder man? I shall always remember his kindness.

My stay in hospital was pleasant up to a point. In fact, only one incident marred my stay. During the second night after the surgery, I was experiencing great pain, and as a result, I summoned the nurse. After a long wait, she finally came—knitting needles in hand.

"Who the hell keep calling 'nurse, nurse'?" she demanded.

"I did."

"What the hell you want?"

"Sleeping pills."

She then handed me my notes, saying, "Can you read?"

"Yes," I said.

"Do you see any damn sleeping pills on that?"

"No!"

"Then keep your damn mouth shut and stop calling 'nurse, nurse' and go to sleep," she said, walking away with her knitting needles in action.

During my convalescence, Dorothy acted as my nurse. At first, she was afraid to negotiate the deep cut left from the surgery, but she soon became proficient at changing the dressing in quick order. One afternoon, Dorothy came home upset. I was annoyed to hear that a friend of mine had told her that he thought I was suffering from cancer. She was comforted when I told her that if it were so, Dr. Farrington would have informed me.

Return to Duty

I returned from the hospital in time to sit the corporal to sergeant examination—which I failed. However, I was happy to have passed two subjects, with only law to sit in April 1969. As it was, only six corporals were successful on the exam. So I was not in bad company in respect to my failure, because such greats as Corporal Ashton Miller and Lance Sergeant Nathaniel Rolle had also suffered the same fate.

Early in September, I returned to duty and was given sedentary work at the Police Personnel Records Office. I had first begun to type at Police Headquarters where I typed the weekly *Force Orders* and other documents that the authorities needed. I had to type letters, memoranda, and disciplinary matters pertaining to officers. I began using two fingers and still type that way. It was called "the hunt-and-peck system," but over the years, my fingers had become so used to the typewriter that I hunted very little and pecked a lot.

On November 4, 1968, good news was heralded throughout the Force. For it was on that day that an increase in police allowances was announced. The detective allowance increased from \$2.25 to \$10.00 per week—but I did not qualify for that allowance. I once requested to be a detective, only to have Watkins inform me that I could not investigate a bad scent in a perfume shop. The plainclothes allowance increased from \$2.50 to \$5.00, and a special allowance—which I did qualify for—of \$5.00 was introduced for every member of the Force, excluding recruits. With Dorothy now employed and a further \$5.00 per week added to my meager salary, we were on our way toward better things. Then came hospital admission number two followed closely by admission number three.

Hospital Admissions Two and Three

On the morning of November 7, I awoke with a high fever and an inability to urinate. I was immediately admitted to the hospital, where the doctor made me sit in hot water to receive relief. During this stay, surgery was not necessary. I suffered from an abscess in the area of my thirteenth part, and it was remedied by sitting in hot water until the pain and swelling subsided.

Like before, Dr. Farrington showed his true form and charged me nothing for his services. I still remember the warning he gave me on my discharge on November 15. "Mr. Burrows," he chided, "stay away from too much peas and rice, macaroni and cheese, potato salad, and eat plenty of fresh vegetables and fruits."

I tried to follow the doctor's advice to the letter, but being a Bahamian, I found it difficult at times. But even in hospital I was in good company, for none other than Assistant Superintendent Cyril Joseph and, yes, commissioner of police Thomas Edwin Clunie fell victims to illnesses around the same time I did and both shared my fate of hospitalization.

Returning to work, I was often sent to the commissioner's residence to deliver and collect important documents relative to his office. During such visits, Mr. Clunie and I would discuss matters of interest, and as a result, he would confide in me. At the expiration of his illness and after he resumed his position, our time together became more frequent. During these times, he shared with me the many brilliant ideas he had for the improvement of the Force.

Others may disagree with my observation, but I think that Mr. Clunie did a lot for the Force as a whole and for me in particular. He treated me "grand." Within three years, I was upgraded from a corporal to a staff sergeant, with a course pending at the Metropolitan Police Training School in Hendon, England.

Owing to the commissioner's illness, his deputy, Mr. Albert Miller, acted in his stead. Mr. Miller was an excellent administrator, and the year, as expected, ended on a high note. He was a man who would have made a first-class commissioner, even though he was not always popular. His philosophy was to remove all the obstacles in the path of progress, and that did not endear him to everyone. However, even his critics would readily admit that he was a cultured, intelligent man, who was full of action and driving ambition.

Just when I thought things were going fine, on May 29, 1969, I was once again admitted to Princess Margaret Hospital for the third time. That same complaint had flared up, and on this occasion, the pain was more severe. Three times I thought was it, and I started to worry whether it was cancerous. I became pessimistic as my mind began to wonder. I was so concerned that death was closing in on me, that when the announcer from ZNS radio interviewed me in my hospital bed during the Hospital Calling show and asked me what song I wished to hear for that Saturday night's broadcast, I requested, "Wait a Little Longer, Please Jesus." It was a popular song at the time, and I thought it was appropriate.

I was afraid to ask Dr. Farrington if my complaint was cancerous, so I was happy when I was discharged on the morning of June 5 at nine thirty. However, I refused to leave until after the refreshments were served. It was at the Princess Margaret Hospital that I discovered the wonderful taste of orange juice and pineapple juice served with crushed ice.

Pray not to get fistula, for it is a very painful ailment. I was told by Dr. Camille Gordon, the doctor who had the good fortune of delivering me, that a woman in labour cannot be worse.

Top Row: Dr. Earl Farrington
Bottom Row: Mr. Carleton Williams and High Commissioner Paul Farquharson

Lessons in Finance

Oh! I almost forgot, in late December, 1968, I made a down payment of one hundred dollars to a real estate company on a piece of property in Eastern Estates. With the total value of the land being just under four thousand dollars and an agreed monthly payment of one hundred dollars, I told Dorothy that we would complete the full payment in record time. On returning to the company to make the second payment, I was sent to a bank where I was given a book and told to report there each month with my payment.

The book showed that sixty-eight dollars went toward the principal and the rest went to interest. Just under the speed of light, I sprinted back to the bank. There I pointed out what I perceived to be an error. This was my first course in finance—and one that I will never forget. It also brought to memory a phrase: "Being poor is no disgrace, but only a put back."

But to my thinking, being put back was a disgrace. Therefore, I contacted an accountant friend who said that the only way I could save money on the transaction was to pay more than one hundred dollars a month, which I did.

New Administration Building

On April, 30, 1969, the Honourable Lynden O. Pindling officially opened the new administrative building. It was the first significant event to occur in the Force in a long time. Previously, the two top floors of this building served as living quarters for recruits with the lower floor serving as the police stores. I resided in this building for the duration of my training.

The building was extensively renovated and the new quarters did much to enhance the working conditions and, indeed, the overall efficiency at Headquarters. Various administrative sections of the force which were previously scattered were brought under one roof.

The top floor housed the commissioner, the deputy commissioner, assistant commissioner, headquarters administration, assistant commissioner, C.I.D., the pay office, staff officer, records office, and dispatch officer.

The second floor housed the Criminal Records Office (CRO) and the Security and Intelligence (SIB) branch. The lower floor housed the force's communications and police stores.

Checkers Shuffle

The publication of *Force Orders* no. 34, dated August 8, 1969, bore glad tidings for me. I was successful in the proficiency examination and was therefore eligible for promotion to sergeant. Shortly after my success, Commissioner Clunie went to England on business. It was during this period that Mr. Miller again acted as commissioner, Mr. Salathiel Thompson acted as deputy, and Mr. Moir replaced the senior assistant commissioner. It was also during this period that I came to appreciate what an exemplary administrator Mr. Moir was. In fact, I found him to be knowledgeable in many areas, including the field of construction.

Shortly after returning from England, Mr. Clunie recruited twenty-four young men as police cadets. A few of those men are still with us, but some I wrote off early in the scheme as a bad investment. Those who remained did well; they were Carlton Cleare, William D. Moss, Matthew Davis, Willard Cunningham, Dereck Musgrove, Prince Bain, Alfred Decosta, Prince Cornish, Joseph Knowles, Clyde Nixon, Alvin Coakley, Arnold Sainville, Carlton Hanna, Aaron Johnson, Ephraim Bullard, Fulton King, and Livingstone Bodie.

Following the visit to England, Mr. Clunie made some strange moves on the Force's checkerboard. His deputy, Mr. Miller, was sent to head the Grand Bahama District on September 22, 1969. This section was later renamed the Northern Region, and the Northern Islands of The Bahamas archipelago formed this boundary. Mr. Salathiel Thompson, who was confirmed as deputy commissioner, on January 1, 1970, succeeded Mr. Miller at Police Headquarters. Mr. Gerald

Bartlett, assistant commissioner of District Headquarters, was later upgraded to the rank of senior assistant commissioner.

Mr. Miller's tenure with the Force spanned some twenty-nine years. He resigned for the prestigious and lucrative position of vice president of the Grand Bahama Port Authority. He subsequently ascended to the position of president. It was a sad day to see when the likes of Mr. Miller exited the Force; as a result, the Force, and indeed The Bahamas, became the poorer. He was a man who believed in standards and would not settle for anything other than the best. Whenever the history of The Bahamas is written, there will definitely be a place for him. He has also since been knighted by Her Majesty, the Queen, and is now addressed as Sir Albert. He came from a humble beginning, a Long Island boy who made good of his life.

In the shuffle, Mr. Moir, assistant commissioner of CID, was posted to Headquarters as the Force's administrative officer. I found Mr. Moir to be a man of superior intelligence, a genuine administrator, and a policeman with long experience of the first order. He was gentlemanly and frank. He was, and will always be, one of the most brilliant and intelligent policeman I have ever met.

My admiration and esteem for Moir only increased with time. He did much to enhance my upward mobility in the Force. It was he, who in December of 1969, called me into his office and said, "All's well [he called me this because of a phrase I often used] because of no fault of yours, you were denied the benefit of a formal education. However, you have the making of a good policeman. But, if you do not do something to improve your educational standard, I am afraid that a sergeant may be your ceiling." That was sad news for me. I asked him for his suggestion, to which he explained the value of reading and the positive effects it has on an individual.

To get me started, Mr. Moir lent me books from his personal library at home, and then he questioned me about what I had read. He would then produce books of a higher standard for me. Each morning, he would take time out of his busy schedule to quiz me on my understanding of what I had read.

Math Problem

Around that same time, a special Trans Education Programme was offered to adults by the government. Mr. Moir advised me to enroll in the programme, and I attempted to. Again, however, the problem was math. Applicants were told to assemble at the Pyfrom Road Secondary School (now called C. I. Gibson Secondary School), and once there, we were asked to express our views on the course and its benefits to our respective fields. The coordinator readily approved my application after completing my interview, but because math was to be an integral part of the course, I withdrew my request, which in retrospect was stupid. Mr. Moir, however, continued to lend encouragement through his constant supply of reading material. This was followed by important case files to study. I enjoyed all the reading and studying and derived much knowledge.

Through Mr. Moir's interest in my education, I developed a thirst for reading that has never stopped. When I travel abroad, one of the first stops I make is to a bookstore. Every night before retiring, I read several passages. Had it not been for Mr. Moir, I would not be in a position to write *Destiny*. If you, therefore, derive any pleasure from reading my presentation, it is due in no small measure to the timely and constructive advice from him, for which I am eternally grateful.

Through reading, I have learned that a great book begins with an idea and a great life with determination. My life may not be great to others, but to me, it has been one of progression and never dull, often exciting, often broke, tired and overworked, but I am reading and learning. Over the years I decided, or my nature decided for me, that I would be a good police officer.

My course in this regard never deviated from the destination I decided on. I experienced many promotional disappointments, yet it was reassuring to know that others had survived. So I thought, keep heart and be happy.

As a result of my illness, the year 1969 ended on a bad note for me. I was given seven days of sick leave on December 30, and thereafter, I suffered discomfort whenever the weather would build up to rain. In fact, my weather predictions were much more accurate than those of the weather forecasters at the Met office.

Another Promotion

Then came January 1970, which brought good fortune: I was promoted to sergeant, and I was very proud of myself. As a result of a salary review which happened in 1969, and my promotion, my annual salary increased from $5,900 to $6,500. It was recognized that police salaries were generally inferior to those enjoyed by other government officers holding posts of, seemingly, comparable responsibilities and status, and all police officers' salaries, from constable to superintendent, were considered for revision.

As a newly promoted sergeant, after receiving the back pay, I sprinted to my bank, where I promptly deposited the money to my account for the property. My behavior brings to mind a phrase I once heard at a meeting I attended where a prominent speaker said, "Boys, you must always remember, ya can't get nothin' fer nothin'." The context that phrase was used in was pathetic, in that, prior to that night, it was said that "you cannot get something for nothing." This was proven to be true in respect to the "rise" in pay, as Chief Superintendent Sydney Minus would have said.

Immediately following the announcement of the salary increase, a new pension provision was made. In essence, it read thus: "By virtue of the above Act, subordinate police officers (i.e. staff sergeants, sergeants, corporals, and constables) will, in future, be required to serve for twenty-five years or until attaining the age of forty-five (whichever shall occur first), before becoming eligible for a pension." Prior to this, the ranks mentioned above were entitled to retire after twenty-one years of service. With this new Act coming into being, my plans were considerably frustrated. You see, it was my intention to retire from the Force after serving twenty-one years, at the relatively young age of thirty-nine. I was then going to embark on a new career somewhere else. To remain after qualifying for a pension, I equated to "paying for one piece of real estate twice."

On May 15, 1970, those in charge were considering the selection of Force personnel to man the sixty-foot Nelson Patrol Craft that was on order in the United Kingdom. Interested officers were asked to apply, and as a result, I grasped the opportunity and submitted my application. What really prompted my application submission, though, was my inside connection that provided me with the information that sergeants would be promoted to inspectors and inspectors to assistant superintendents. I reluctantly withdrew my request after being told that "slow growth is good growth." I was also warned not to become dazzled by the promise of inspectorate promotion. Instead, I should learn the job properly and wait for the appointed time to be promoted.

At the time of my promotion to sergeant, the commissioner published a special list of named officers that he said had been given accelerated seniority. A substantial number of those officers selected for promotion were given accelerated seniority as an incentive and as recognition of their high ratings in the Promotion Board's estimation. I was one of those officers selected.

Among the other sergeants receiving accelerated promotions were Sergeant Bernard K. Bonamy, Sergeant Nathaniel Rolle, Corporal Henry Thurston, Sergeant Kendal Lightbourn, and Corporal Granville Antonio. There were four others who, for one reason or another, fell by the wayside. Mr. Bonamy, however, pulled away from the pack, even though he was only seventh on the list. I suppose that while the others played cards and dominoes in the Police Canteen, Mr. Bonamy played the books. He had a sophisticated, urban mind, when dealing with aspects of leadership. It has been said that "long-lasting fame comes to but a few." Today, I am thankful to God for allowing me to be among the few.

The year 1970 was a year of jubilation for certain members of the Force. During my almost thirty-two years of service, I had not seen a larger number of police officers of various ranks promoted. The promotions were as follows: one deputy commissioner, one senior assistant commissioner, five superintendents, ten assistant superintendents, twelve chief inspectors, seventeen inspectors, thirty-four sergeants, seventy-one corporals, and many acting appointments of various ranks. All these promotions were given in an authorized establishment of 1,070 people, with a strength of 906. In respect to overseas courses, not fewer than thirty-four officers attended police colleges in England during 1970.

Then there was the news that the great warrior, Errington Washington Isaac Watkins, an officer of the law who had risen to the rank of deputy superintendent of police, had traded his police appointment for the chairmanship of the United Bahamian Party. Someone once asked my good friend Watkins, while chairman, if he was going to run candidates against a group of men who had broken away from the ruling party and were calling themselves the “Free PLPs.” Watkins humorously replied, “I will be running candidates against Free PLPs and slave PLPs.”

The year 1971 proved to be more exciting than the previous one. In early January, a selection was made for the newly formed Police Marine Division, the forerunner of the Royal Bahamas Defence Force. On the evening of the first Friday in March, 1971, the commissioning ceremony for the Police Patrol Boats was triumphantly held. Mr. Clunie, that much maligned man, sat alongside the Honourable Prime Minister and Mrs. Lynden Pindling to witness the magnificent ceremony. A multitude of people assembled in the gardens of the British Colonial Hotel for the launch on that glorious day. The setting was ideal, with the police band playing music appropriate to the occasion. Shortly after the sun’s setting, the country’s chief law enforcement officer mounted the podium to begin the ceremony.

As usual, few things went according to plan. During his speech, Mr. Clunie announced, “Honourable Prime Minister, distinguished ladies and gentlemen, if you were to look behind, you will see riding majestically at anchor, your fleet of newly equipped patrol crafts.” An English officer was supposed to turn on the lights to illuminate the boats and the Marines in their immaculate white uniforms. But when all assembled turned to face the harbour, all they saw was darkness. Clunie, who had thus far in the ceremony given a good account of himself, growled, "Find that man X." Mr. X, who well knew Clunie's temperament, ascertained the problem and had it fixed in short order. By this time, however, the commissioner's temper had flared and his pride was dented. When he caught up with the offending officer sometime later, one of the kindest things he told him was, "I am an Englishman, only Christ knows where you came from!"

Despite that little hitch, the commissioner later wrote that the commissioning ceremony was the proudest moment in his long policing career. The officer who failed to flip the switch at the appropriate time however, was never forgiven for his moment of blunder.

With the commissioning ceremony behind him, and as Mr. Clunie would often say, "nothin' should stand still," he began to trouble the promotion waters. After the troubling, however, I received only a half blessing. I was made a staff sergeant, but I was expecting to be upgraded to inspector. My disappointment was a result of information I read in the police publication: "The rank of staff sergeant and chief superintendent shall be given to those sergeants and superintendents, who have served faithfully over the years, and who are about to retire from the Force, lacking the necessary qualifications and general merit to further ascend the promotion ladder."

What depressed me even more was that sergeants below me in seniority had surpassed me and been made inspectors. Then I examined the other two sergeants who had been made staff sergeants, and I found that their credentials were not too glistening. After my summation, I thought I was not in good company, for both gentlemen had come from backgrounds similar to mine and their formal educations had stopped at the secondary level, where students were more concerned with manners and religion than they were with ideas. To add insult to injury, on the following day, I met and was congratulated by the now deceased Assistant Superintendent Fletcher Johnson. He was known as "Beaver," He reminded me of the staff sergeant promotion.

I approached the deputy commissioner and revealed my concern to him. Mr. Thompson said, "Burrows, I told them to give you nothing, we have a plan for you, which will be revealed in due time. You know nothing about policing; therefore, you will have to go from Headquarters and prove yourself as a man fit for khaki."

Like a dog without a bone, I departed the deputy's office. I found solace that afternoon in Dorothy's arms. On many such occasions thereafter, she lent me a shoulder to rest on and an ear to vent my frustrations to. I have known many men who sought comfort from the bottle, while others took up temporary residences in bathrooms where they kept close companionship with rolls of toilet paper, only to find that life must go on.

In early May, 1971, there was gossip throughout the Force portending Mr. Clunie's intended departure from the police service. Shortly thereafter, it became a reality. Then the speculation started. Which one of the deputies would succeed him? But that's politics, so let's move on.

On the afternoon of June 13, 1971, at the Prince George Dock, the Clunies—Thomas, Janette, and their two sons—were given a grand "send off," as the departed commissioner described it on a ship's postcard he sent me from Bermuda. After the ceremonies, the senior officers and I were feted in a reserved room aboard the cruise ship *Oriana* until it was time to depart. With Mr. Clunie gone and Mr. Miller acting in his stead until a successor had been chosen, I began a twelve-week vacation leave starting July 2. By this point in time, I had completed the full payment on my property; I also had in my possession an approved plan for the construction of a dwelling home. I was becoming tired of toting water from the corner faucet, and after all, I was moving up in the ranks, even though, for the moment, the future seemed dark.

I spent my holiday cleaning up my property and visiting banks, with negative results. On visiting each bank, I was given the same sad story: "Sorry, but you do not qualify for the loan of $22,500." I was asked to produce a third of the cost or to have construction done to the value of a third, neither of which I was able to provide. After all my efforts had failed, I decided to build my home in stages. I paid my contractor six thousand dollars for stages one and two. I then ran out of cash, so I circled the banks again, only to be met with the same barriers as before. This time, however, I was more determined. I exerted more energy and effort into my pursuit, but eventually I was forced to suffer the same rejection. Those of you who may remember the story of "King Bruce and the Spider" will also recall that after many defeats he finally succeeded in overcoming his enemies. With that story in mind, I once again proceeded on round three with the intent to convince some banker of my plight—but again, without results.

Then suddenly I struck fortune. Feeling completely rejected, I had been wending my way along Shirley Street after being let down by a loan officer at Barclay's Bank. Then I heard my name being called. I turned around and there was my cousin, Mrs. Ida Hanna (nee Farquharson), whom I had not seen for a number of years. After the usual greetings, she asked me how life was treating me. "Not too good," I said. Then I shared with her my plight.

Ida, who was in the banking circles, asked, "Rodney, why you didn't let me know?"

Later that day, she sent me to see a charming woman named Mrs. Beryl Adams at the Finance Corporation of The Bahamas Limited. She instructed a man, who answered to the name of McGee, to process my application for the loan, and thereafter, I was on my way.

Rodney Burrows, Constable 1961, Corporal 1968 and Sergeant 1970

Transfer to Central Division

On my return to work, I was told that in early 1972, I was to be transferred to Central Division where it was hoped that I would learn some policing before proceeding on to Hendon, England for a course of study.

The Force's ninth commissioner, Mr. John Hedley Hindmarsh, was appointed on August 5, 1971, and he was to serve for two years. The reason being that when The Bahamas became independent, a Bahamian commissioner was to be in place. Shortly after his arrival, Mr. Albert Miller, that giant of a policeman, was about to make his departure from the Force, leaving Mr. Thompson as the likely candidate to replace Mr. Hindmarsh in two years. With my departure from Headquarters set for February 1, 1972, I conditioned my mind for that which lay ahead. From the gossipmongers, I received nothing but bad news. They informed me that, according to those in authority at Central, I would be shown nothing, because I had received several promotions and did little or nothing to merit them.

In the middle of January, 1972, the deputy commissioner Thompson promised to send assistant superintendent of police Alphonso Marshall to head the Central Division. He informed me that Mr. Marshall was a fine officer who would help me a great deal, and he surely did.

At eight in the morning on Monday, February 1, 1972, I reported for duty at Central and was greeted by those who held the reign of power: Assistant Superintendent Cyril Joseph; Sergeant Eddison Seymour; Sergeant Ashton Miller; Sergeant Vernon Grant; Lance Sergeant Chesterfield Bynoe; and Corporals Michael Ellis, Merril Duford, George Cooper; and Constable

Wendell Taylor. Women Constables Clarice Stuart and Bridget Gibson were the clerk and bookkeeper of Records respectively. There was also an inspector who shall remain nameless.

At Central, I met a solid team and what the gossipmongers had alleged about my coming was not evident. The first person to come to my assistance was Corporal Ellis. On my arrival, he handed me a notcbook with all the necessary charges drafted therein. Next, the inspector gave me twelve court dockets with a number of charges recorded thereon. I went to Central with an open mind and was well received.

Then came Friday, at five p.m., when a party was held in my honour at Headquarters. While the merriment was in progress, the gathering was informed that three prisoners had escaped from the cells at Central, one being the infamous Victor Storr. That news brought the party to an abrupt halt, and I immediately left for Central Station. When I arrived at Central Police Station, the place was buzzing with senior officers and other ranks as well as news reporters. The mere fact that Victor Storr was one of the escapees triggered top news headlines. Shortly thereafter, some of the most daring robberies would soon occur; banks would be at the top of his crime spree.

Two days later, Victor pulled off one of the most daring robberies of his time. He entered a bank dressed in woman's clothing, high-heeled shoes, and drop earrings I am told. He jumped over the counter of the financial institution and, with a gun in one hand and a pillowcase in the other, he ordered that the pillowcase be filled with paper money only, as coins were too heavy. During the robbery, Victor told a frightened teller not to stuff the pillowcase too tight because it might burst. After his capture, Victor confirmed that the story about the pillowcase was true. He may be termed the "Dillinger" of the seventies.

With the passing of time, I finally grasped the work and was getting on top of things when a chief inspector, who seemed to have a dislike for the inspector, arrived on the scene. I can assure you that the feelings the chief inspector had for the inspector were reciprocated, and I was the one who was caught in the middle. So I had to stand my ground. I found both men to be treacherous, but the chief inspector, who had a little more experience at the game, was devious as well. He never did anything to correct things because he would have others carry the blame. He was one you could trust to take the wrong view on any subject. To support my observation, I shall relate to you two incidents.

Prior to the arrival of the chief inspector, the inspector was known as the divisional inspector and I was the divisional officer. On the arrival of the chief inspector, however, the inspector's status changed to my position, and I was made the divisional sergeant. The ambitious inspector detested his demotion, and as a result, he requested that I deal with the matters that he and the chief inspector should have dealt with. For example, the inspector should have handed over all the complaints to the chief inspector, and he should have briefed him on all outstanding matters. But the jobs were left to me. Both inspector and chief inspector avoided each other as though the other suffered from some incurable disease. On the chief inspector's second day, I informed him that I was in possession of the complaints and the keys to the found property room and that I was available at his convenience to hand them over to him, or for him to inspect them at any time. He said, "Shorty, I just reach,(arrived) and I will let you know when I am ready."

One week later, on my return from making my rounds, I came upon the chief inspector and a sergeant talking in Bank Lane. I was surprised when he addressed me. "Hey, Shorty. I was here now for over two weeks and I have yet to see the outstanding complaints."

I immediately told him, "Chief, I reminded you on more than one occasion of the complaints." He then mumbled something that made no sense before I walked away. An hour later, the chief inspector saw me alone and told me that it was not me he was after but the inspector. I told him to fight his battle with the inspector and to leave me alone.

Shortly after incident number one, the chief inspector requested that I collect the uniform from a senior constable who refused to work. The constable, he said, was seen sitting on a wall in the Farrington Road area and it was necessary that I move quickly. I informed the chief inspector that the station's vehicle was in the garage. To this, he said, "Shorty, you is a man with plenty pull at Headquarters, and if you request a car be sent, they would comply." I made the request, got a car from headquarters and brought the constable and his uniform to Central.

The chief inspector, by this time, was at Eastern Police Station checking found property with the intent to find something short to get some poor policeman in trouble over. Because it was payday, the constable, who turned out to be my recruit mate, asked to be taken to the bank while I collected sand from Malcolm Park to fix the cells. Coincidentally, the constable and I both banked at the, then, CIBC at the Potter's Cay branch. While en route to the bank and park, the constable driving the car stopped at Eastern Police Station to let the chief inspector and the offending constable talk. We then continued on our journey.

I do not recall in minute details what happened at the trial, but the constable was seen by the deputy commissioner and the constable told him that he did not work because his uniform was taken from him. Even though the constable had stopped working prior to his uniform being taken, he was fined and allowed to retain his job. On the constable's return to work, the chief inspector inquired from me the reason for him not being fired. I told him of the deputy commissioner's ruling that he was the only person who could direct the taking of an officer's uniform, and that divisional personnel should not take for granted that it meant automatic dismissal if an officer absented himself from duty. Be that as it may, I think that the deputy commissioner was only trying to make a point. I thought that the constable should have been fired.

Given that explanation, the chief inspector became furious. In a burst of anger, he said, "The next time these fellows don't come for weeks to work, I am not going to hurt my head. Here it is, we caught this no good man and they letting him go, talking foolishness about taking uniforms. I am tired of this foolishness." Then, as if he did not understand, he suddenly calmed down and said, "Shorty, who again you said send —— back to work?"

"The deputy commissioner," I answered.

"And why he did not fire him, you mind repeating?"

"Because we took his uniform without authority."

Then there was a long pause. After recollecting his thoughts, he continued his questioning. "Who took his uniform?"

"Me, on your instructions," I replied.

Then there was a longer pause, during which time he was putting together his cover story. It was then that I lost all respect for him. "Shorty," he finally said with a cunning grin, "you sure it was me?"

"Yes," I replied.

"You sure it was not Marshall?

"Yes," I answered.

I went to great lengths to refresh his memory by reminding him how he had asked me to obtain the car from the garage and that he and the constable had actually spoken at Eastern Police Station. At the conversation's end, the chief inspector said that he was going to check his diary later that day because it was his belief that he was on casual leave. Today, it makes me bitter to write this passage and to see a man disassociate himself from instructions he gave to me an "inferior" in rank. Allow me now to mention, briefly, my reason for using that noun in respect to the inspector. Incidentally, he had "diarrhea" of the mouth, and oh, how he loved to talk and show off.

One day, a report came in to Central that a bomb had been planted in the Churchill Building and was expected to explode in ten minutes. On learning the bomb's reported location, it immediately meant something to the inspector (for this would give the top executives of the country the opportunity to observe my overzealous colleague in action). He was on the telephone when the news came in, and with whom I do not know, but he ran out of the office leaving the phone off its cradle and shouting, "Staff, (short for staff sergeant) come quick." With me in tow, we sprinted down Bank Lane as if we were to receive pearls at the other end. Therefore I was surprised when the inspector came to a sudden stop on seeing a beautiful girl—and then instigated a lively conversation. Naturally I was startled, for this was the first bomb scene I was to attend and then this abrupt conversation commenced.

They conversed until the commissioner's car passed by a few seconds later with its flag fluttering and headed toward the Churchill Building. Without a departing word, the man leaped and ran across Bay Street as if he were shot from a cannon, all the while shouting, "Are you with me, staff?" Well, for a start, I was afraid to run across the heavy stream of traffic as he had fled across its path. This may be somewhat difficult to believe, but I was told that the inspector was in place to open the car door for the commissioner on his arrival. The call about the bomb turned out to be a prank. Let me now take you further along the path of destiny.

There was never any scarcity of work at Central. The officers and inspectors saw to it that I was made to circle Bay Street, Woodes Rogers Wharf, and Prince George Dock at least three times a day, along with a number of other chores. At that time, the areas were bustling with activity, the busiest being the fish and straw markets, Bay Street with peddlers hawking their wares, and the market range where the vagrants roamed. All the loose things seemed to drift down to the sea, and Freeman and James Dean, among others, were always present. There were also straw vendors spreading their wares along the sidewalks, the diving boys/men were at Prince George Dock, and the list goes on.

Arrangements for my attendance at the Metropolitan Police Training School, Hendon, England, were finalized. While I was excited to have been selected to receive the training, which was my first opportunity to study abroad, I was concerned about leaving my family for five months. Fortunately, we were still living in close proximity to Dorothy's parents who assured me that they would take care of my family. My daughters Val and Ally were then eight and six years old respectively. I was fortunate as I was granted an In-Service-Training Award, which meant that I would continue to receive my salary as well as a monthly allowance for the duration of the training. My salary therefore would take care of my obligations to my family with the allowance covering my expenses while in England.

As time drew near for me to depart for London, I became excited and approached two inspectors who would have attended the Hendon course last. The first spoke about a new book entitled *The Theft Act* and ended by saying, "If you get past that, you will be all right." The second inspector, who was as unpredictable as the English weather, gave me a lecture on subjects ranging from the British Isles to where popcorn may be purchased—but nothing about the course. On a positive note, I was approached two days prior to my departure by Mr. Paul Rupert Thompson, a veteran police officer.

"Burrows," he said, "I understand you will be attending a course in England, and you will need white shirts. At home, I have two that you may have. You are required to wash and hang them up, after which they may be worn without having to be ironed."

I was very surprised by Mr. Thompson's kindness because he had rarely spoken to me before. I knew that he was an excellent detective from the many conversations that I had overheard about him. Mr. Thompson, as the saying goes, "slept, ate, and dreamt policing." After I got to know him better, I had to concur with the observations of others. It was a sad day when this exemplary officer decided to exit the Force at a time when he still had so much to offer.

Top Row: Salathiel Thompson, Stanley Moir, Alonzo Butler
Middle Row: Ashton Miller, Errington "Bumpy" Watkins, Leifred Johnson
Bottom Row: Alphonso Marshall, Edney Johnson

Police Overseas Course, Hendon, England

At six p.m. on September 22, 1972, I boarded a British Overseas Airways Corporation (BOAC) aircraft for London. Travelling on the same flight were two government employees: Mr. Reginald Wood, financial secretary; and Mr. Othneil Watson, treasurer. We engaged in brief conversation and they told me that if I needed any assistance, I could contact them. About two and a half hours later, the plane landed in Bermuda. Shortly thereafter, we were once again airborne, and to my amazement, an announcement came over the intercom saying that a movie would be shown shortly. How can this thing be? I thought. To show a movie on an airplane at thirty thousand feet sounded ludicrous. However, I waited patiently to see how the screen and projector would be erected. Then suddenly, a screen appeared, the lights in the cabin dimmed, and, with the aid of a headset, I was enjoying a movie.

At the film's end, I observed the breaking of dawn, which to me was difficult to comprehend. At this point in my life, I had no knowledge of the time zones. (It was not until some years later, in my thirst for knowledge, that I fully understood the logic behind that which, hitherto, appeared to be puzzling.) As we flew into day, with the rays of dawn fast appearing, breakfast was served. Then once the utensils were collected, we were asked to prepare for the descent. In short order, the blue sky that I was accustomed to disappeared; I was not to see it again until my return to The Bahamas some five months later.

The plane having landed, I observed what appeared to be smoke emanating from the mouths and nostrils of the people gathered. As it was my first time entering a cold country, and not knowing what to expect, I attempted to exit the plane without an overcoat. I hurried back into the aircraft to don my cheap overcoat and then I stepped boldly into the famous terminal of London's Heathrow Airport.

Once inside, I became completely confused; I believe it was because of the multitude of people going to-and-fro. On two occasions, I found myself following fellow passengers who were connecting with other aircrafts. Eventually, I was led to the area where my luggage awaited me, minus, of course, the passengers with whom I had travelled.

With a suitcase in each hand and an overnight bag hung over my shoulder, I struggled to an awaiting customs officer who inspected the contents of my luggage. The officer was kind and helpful to me, and in minutes, I found myself facing a huge crowd of people, some of them bearing placards with names written on them. In vain, I carefully read each placard over and again. Finally in disbelief, I concluded that there was no representative from the British Council to meet me. I later realized that I misread the journeying instructions. I was to have taken a train to London's Victoria Station where I was to be met by a representative of the British Council and apprised of the arrangements in respect to accommodations.

My predicament, I quickly reasoned, should be resolved if a police officer was apprised thereof. My attention then began to focus on uniforms. Soon among the hustle and fast movement of human traffic, I spotted an approaching constable. I presented my case to the officer. Then I listened as the English bobby spoke into his pocket radio set and related my pathetic story to his superior at the Airport Police Station.

About five minutes later, a police inspector appeared on the scene. After the usual greetings, he assisted with the conveyance of my belongings to a police patrol car. Next, I was driven to the police station, where I was fed and made to feel comfortable. For the exceptional services rendered, I offered to make a small financial contribution, but it was flatly refused. So I offered a number of cigars that an employee of the Paradise Island Casino had given me. I must confess that the cigars were not a good quality. They were packed so tightly, that both sides of your jaw connected with each draw. On each cigar was written the word "Casino," and I presumed they were given to people for the asking, which also suggests that they were readily available to those unfortunate gamblers to chew on, to avoid biting their tongues while losing their money.

After thanking and bidding my new acquaintances farewell, I was once again placed into a patrol car; its destination was the Metropolitan Police Training School in Hendon. The distance between Heathrow and Hendon was great, and I was asked not to volunteer information about the means by which I travelled to Hendon. To express my fond gratitude to the patrol car driver, I offered him another one of those infamous no name brand cigars, which he was grateful for.

Once I was deposited at Hendon, I thought that all was well. To my dismay, I had to overcome another hurdle in the figure of a guard who denied my admittance. According to him, officers attending the Sixty-fifth Overseas Course were not due until two p.m. on Sunday. I arrived too early. Finally, with the assistance of a convincing tongue and the benefit of an unnamed cigar, I was allowed admittance into that damp and dreary institution of learning and assigned a room.

After resting for an hour, I soon became hungry. Naturally, I was forced to make yet another call on the guard, who directed me to the town of Golders Green, where he thought good food might be had. My questions now: where the hell was Golders Green and how was I to get there? The guard told me to take the tube (an underground train) from Colindale and exit at the fourth stop.

Confused, I set off in the direction of Colindale, pondering in the drizzle and cold the reality of an underground train hitting me. In the movies, I had seen overland trains but no underground trains! What this guard was talking about seemed preposterous. Despite my confusion, I nevertheless pressed on in the direction of the Colindale train station. On arriving, my attention was drawn to the massive crowd of people rushing to-and-fro in their endeavours to exit and board the fast-moving trains. I observed this for a short while before I commenced reading the many signs posted throughout the terminal. Then it was time, I thought, for me to venture a little further.

So I approached the saleswoman at the ticket window and ordered a round-trip fare to Golders Green. On receipt of the ticket, I produced a handful of English coins from which the cashier took, what I assumed, to be the correct amount. In the not too distant past, the English used pounds, shillings, and pence, but the currency had since been converted to a decimal system. Still in circulation, however, were the two shillings (ten new pence), one-six shilling (five new pence), and one-six pence piece (two and a half pence). I was familiar with the currency just described, but other types were foreign.

People walked at a fast pace in England. There was also speed and efficiency in all their transactions, hence my decision to pay in the unusual manner by allowing the salesperson to pick out the proper coin from the coffer in my hand.

With the aid of the ticket, I was allowed through the barrier and then to the trains. If my memory is correct, Colindale was on the black line, and I did not need to change trains from Colindale to Golders Green. Once seated, I began to observe what the others were doing, and I quickly came to the realization that the English observed more and spoke less. As a result, I was somewhat reluctant to ask a question. Then a black man boarded the train at Hendon Central and I felt a little more comfortable. On entering, he remarked, "What say there homeboy." I recognized the Jamaican accent right away.

And I replied, "All's well!"

At the end of a lively discussion on the art of riding the trains all day for a single fare, if that was your desire, I got off at Golders Green.

Not knowing east from west or north from south, I set off in search of food. Like the Bethlehem star, I came to rest in an Italian restaurant where a variety of food awaited. Having placed my order, I then fancied a drink. The waiter was taken aback with my ignorance on the drinking laws in England. In 1972, it was an offence to serve liquor after ten or ten thirty p.m. and believe me, over there, that law was followed to the letter. It was, however, five minutes before the bar was to close. After much pleading, and almost in tears from the cold, I was finally given a stiff drink of gin and tonic with a twist of lime. My appetite would have been appeased further had the bartender acceded to my request for seconds and maybe thirds, but according to him, he had to protect his license. Man, I thought, was a selfish creature. While I concentrated heavily on my pleasure and comfort, my friend the bartender had his license to think about.

The trains ceased operations at midnight on Saturdays, and I only just caught the last one to Colindale. At the gate of my new abode stood the guard, who was happy to see someone with whom he might converse. Because of the cold, however, I did not tarry long. On my departure, I gave him another cigar. The following morning with the crack of dawn, I arose—but the cold drove me back under layers of blankets. An hour or so later, a battle ensued between my hunger and the cold, with my hunger distantly outpointing the elements. Common sense, therefore, dictated that I wash my face, feet, and hands, and then get on the road in search of grub. From all indications, however, it would appear that the night guard omitted to mention my presence to his relief. For at the gate, I was asked to account for my being on the compound. After a long explanation and the passing of a long cigar, to my credit, I had recruited another friend.

On this outing, I disembarked at Hendon Central where I had a breakfast of Kentucky Fried Chicken and hot tea. The day being Sunday, I walked around looking at the displays in the windows until it was time to return to the school, where I was to meet the supervisors and other students.

When I arrived at Hendon, the students were being shown around the campus. After a lengthy explanation, minus the famous cigar, I was told to join the group. In all, there were sixteen of us from ten different countries. Among the group was a station sergeant from a Caribbean island, and from the time my eyes beheld that soul, I concluded that he was a miser and a show-off. He was a tall, heavyset man, with a mouth as flat as money. True to form, his looks coincided with his attitude.

There were Africans, Asians, four of us from the Caribbean, and two females. The lone Chinese, Mak Su-Ming, who said his grandmother was born in Nassau, stuck with those of us from the Caribbean. We participated in a course on general police duties. The curriculum included current affairs, forensic evidence and law with specific reference on a relatively new piece of legislation, The Thief Act, 1968.

Each morning, except when classes were held at Hendon, we visited places of interest. The group was bused to Peel House on Regent Street in London, where we joined the recruits at the Metropolitan Police Training School. On weekends, we were free to do as we pleased: study, go into London, visit friends, or stay in our rooms and sleep. At first I travelled to London with the Caribbean boys, but this was short-lived when I discovered that one of my new friends only had train money but had nevertheless developed a fine taste for beers. All was not the same for Gene Pestina, my lawyer friend from Dominica, who was the same as me, as he would spend his last coin on a friend.

Exceptionally good to us were the families of Rotary members in Hendon. Once a week, we were taken to their respective homes for food, drinks, and entertainment. Most times, we were asked to sing for whatever we received. Does that sound familiar? Yes, little Tommy Tucker, poor fellow, had to "sing for his supper."

The room I resided in while at Hendon had newspapers from around the world stuck between cracks and creases in the window. The building was supposed to be demolished years before, but because of labour unrest, this was prevented. It is my understanding, however, that my class was the last one to have occupied that cold, damp structure. When I visited Hendon some two years later to see Sergeants Ashton Miller and Joseph Major, they were residing in new quarters a short distance from the former.

Before journeying to England for this course, I had the pleasure of meeting an Englishman named Peter Skinner. Our introduction came as a result of Mr. Ken Westbury, the general manager of the pest control firm Rentokil and a member of the Senior Officers' Mess, asking that his supervisor, Peter, be taken to the Sergeants' Mess for a game of darts. It is said that one good deed deserves another, and I have discovered that a good deed never goes unpaid. Trust my judgment. Peter, having been told of my impending course, wrote to his parents in Surrey requesting that I be allowed to visit their home whenever the occasion arose. With this in mind, I telephoned the Skinners and introduced myself. They assured me of their approval and that I was at liberty to visit at all times.

Before venturing further, however, I thought it expedient to learn more about London and its surrounding areas. Some Saturdays, after my unpleasant chore of washing laundry, I would set off for London, alone of course, to visit the museums and other places of interest. While on the topic of washing, let me share with you a secret. Before I left for England, Dorothy had bought me new white undergarments and new black socks. Prior to this, I had never washed clothes, and yes, you guessed correctly—my first attempt was *disastrous*. Into the bucket I placed the white and black clothing. Dorothy had no sympathy for my stupidity when I wrote and told her. She wrote this reply: "Rodney, in your case, looks are not deceiving; because you resemble a fool does not mean you have to be a fool." Thereafter, I learned that white and black don't mix—sometimes!

During my stay in England, I got lost more times than Alice did wandering around Wonderland. My being lost occurred so frequently that an entire volume can be written. On one occasion while travelling to London, at a time when I thought I understood the routes of the trains, I ended up at the end of the line in a small town named Modern. While sitting on the train, a conductor appeared and asked me my intended destination. When I told him Charing Cross, he replied, "Bloody hell! Well how did you get all the way down here?"

"On this train," I told him.

We both laughed. After which, he explained that at a certain time in the day, the train divides in two. So twelve coaches leave Colindale, and on reaching a stop called Euston, the train divides. The first six or last six coaches go to London, and the other six go elsewhere. Well, in my case, I should have read the board to ascertain the difference. Needless to say, I had to learn the difficult way. For the conductor's kindness and for putting me back on track, I gave him a cigar. Naturally, he was overjoyed.

The time came when I thought that I had mastered the train routes, and therefore, I decided it was time to ride the double-decker buses. I would perch like a bird on the top deck and ride for hours, taking in the various scenes. Oh! England is a pretty place. The gardens are breathtaking, the museums are massive and informative, the cathedrals are monumental, and the statues of great men readily remind you of those who helped to shape the course of history. England's rich culture is everywhere. Even though the English are a much disciplined people, once you win their confidences, you have friends for life.

As with the trains, I got accustomed to the buses, and then it was time to venture further—to Lingfield, Surrey, to visit the Skinners. I was scheduled to arrive on a Saturday; therefore, I telephoned on Friday to inform my hosts. To reach Surrey, you have to travel by an overland train from the Victoria Train Station. Without much trouble, I arrived at my destination. The Skinners treated me grandly, and as a result, the next weekend I took a change of clothing with me. The Skinners took me around to visit the shops, pubs, and other places of interest.

In Lingfield, there was also a village club where members were permitted to entertain guests. There, they took me to a dance, and believe me, as bad a dancer as I might be, I became an instant hit with the crowd. The ladies thought that I had taken special lessons because of the brilliance of many of my extraordinary moves. With that amount of praise, I came to appreciate the indisputable value of the stimulants entitled gin and tonic. A few puffs on a Casino cigar and a crowd of villagers, who were not accustomed to seeing an island boy dance, spelled out popularity in Lingfield, where I had yet to see another black person. At first, I felt like a fly in a glass of milk, but with the passing of time and the kindness of the people, I soon settled down.

On his resignation from the Force, after serving as the commissioner of police between 1963 and 1968 in The Bahamas, Mr. Nigel Godfrey Morris, with whom I had worked closely with at Police Headquarters, extended an invitation to me to visit him should I ever get to England. Prior to his appointment in The Bahamas, Mr. Morris had risen to the prestigious rank of deputy inspector general of police and was well known at Hendon where I was a student. Midway through my twenty-week course, I contacted Mr. Morris. Two weeks later, he and his wife Rosetta appeared at Hendon, picked me up, and drove me to Sloane Square, a posh area of London, where they resided. A scrumptious meal was served, after which Mr. Morris took me on a tour of London and then back to my place of abode. I was asked to call whenever I felt like it.

Two weeks before the Christmas break, I was summoned to the course's supervisor's office and was given a message from Mr. Morris inviting me to dinner during the Christmas holidays. Further, the supervisor wanted to know where Morris and I had met. I am sure I rose a few notches in his estimation after that telephone message. I was certainly viewed by many as a celebrity.

A fortnight later, I visited the Skinners again. On this occasion, they introduced me to their grocers Mr. and Mrs. Sydney Jeffreys, who in turn introduced me to Mr. and Mrs. Ron Robertson and their son, Gary. The Jeffreys had no children; instead, they had and cherished a dog named Rumba. That animal received excellent care at the hands of Syd and Kath Jeffreys. Syd was a short, chubby fellow with not much schooling, but he was endowed with a wealth of common sense and experience. After a drink or two of whisky, Syd would talk politics for hours. But his dear wife, Kath, who was fun to be with, disliked politics. She did, however, cherish ABB (AnyBody's Brand of liquor). Then I met Tommy and Marjorie Wallis, a fine couple with an only daughter named Susan. They introduced me to several of their friends. Oh my! They were happy times.

The first two females to attend the overseas course at Hendon were from the Seychelles. They were both constables. And while Constable Confeit was bright and pretty, Baker was dark and only "so-so" in the looks department. Never in my life have I seen two women given so much attention. The guys would form a queue to pull out their chairs at mealtimes. Suffice it to say that we were there for five months, and that is a very long time.

At Christmas, we were required to relocate to the Commonwealth House in London. I resided in Surrey, where each morning I was served tea and crackers in bed. That's right, in *bed*. Many times I pinched myself and asked, is this me? The answer, of course, came back yes, it was.

Classes at Hendon reconvened in January of 1973, and it was time for attachment to the English Police Forces. Three others and I were sent to Bristol, England, and Bridge End in Wales. In my company was a chap from Africa who had hitherto not seen the sea. When his eyes beheld the channel at Bristol, he was ever so pleased. Frank Shivers, staff officer to the commissioner of police for Bristol, was our guide. After collecting us from the train station and endeavouring to park the boss' car in the garage, he dented the fender. Listening to Frank explain that slight mishap was like listening to an intensive discourse on psychology. His explanation for the cause of the mishap was not carelessness but "an error of judgment."

The accommodations at Bridge End were not the best. There was no heating in the rooms, only a contraption that resembled a hot plate. For warmth, you had to insert a ten pence coin into the hot plate contraption, and if you were not asleep in short order, you had to insert another and then another until you fell asleep. To me, it was punishment of the first order.

Sergeant Rodney Burrows, far right, other course participants and facilitators, Metropolitan Police Training School, Hendon, January 1973

Sergeant Rodney Burrows, second left and other course participants at a police station, Bridge End, Wales, January, 1973.

Sergeant Rodney Burrows, second left, back row, other course participants and instructors, Metropolitan Police Training School, Hendon, 9 February, 1973.

The following morning, we ate breakfast at a small restaurant not far from where we slept. The waitress who served us appeared to be in her early seventies and watched our every move. As at Bristol, we were taken to meet the powers that be by a sergeant from the training school. The day was well spent, and the police and sergeant assigned to us even bought us our favorite drinks. The Welch, like Bahamians, enjoyed their drinks. I was in familiar territory and enjoyed every moment of it. After all, it was nearing the time for me to bid England farewell.

The next morning, the old woman who had waited on us the previous day asked me, "You all come looking for work aye?"

"No," I hastily replied. "I would rather be in jail in Nassau than be free to live over here." We both smiled. She was a sweet old woman who said that she would welcome a change from such terrible weather.

My overall visit to Bristol and Wales was very rewarding and afforded me the opportunity to interact with English police officers and observe their method of policing. I was, however, beginning to feel homesick and wanted to go home. More than anything, I longed to see my wife and children. So my return to Hendon was one step closer to home.

Once at Hendon, it was time to prepare for the graduation ceremony. Therefore, we were surprised when we were told to submit an essay entitled, "London and Its People." With all examinations completed and everything restored to their original states, we waited with much anticipation for the day of our farewell dinner. Finally, on the eighth day of February, 1973, we were called to order. In eighth place, with sixty-seven percent, Staff Sergeant Rodney Ador Burrows. A brilliant student I never professed to be. I did, however, my best.

During the consumption of our last supper, the president of Rotary International presented me with a book entitled *London Through the Looking Glass*, by Ted Smart. It was for my first place effort on my essay, "London and Its People." I was very pleased to receive such a prize. It certainly made up for my eighth place finish overall at my class performance. On completion of the speeches, we danced the night away to the sounds of a live band.

The following morning, I departed Hendon in the company of my friends Kath and Sydney Jeffreys; our destination, Lingfield, Surrey. That same night, at the home of the Jeffreys, they held a farewell party in my honour. Late into the night, I kissed my invited friends goodbye and thanked them for their kindness and for accepting me in their company. The following morning, I boarded a British Overseas Airways Corporation (BOAC) aircraft for New Providence.